Deterring the Drinking Driver

Deterring the Drinking Driver

Legal Policy and Social Control

Revised and Updated Edition

H. Laurence Ross
University of New Mexico

LexingtonBooks
D.C. Heath and Company
Lexington, Massachusetts
Toronto

Library of Congress Cataloging in Publication Data

Ross, H. Laurence (Hugh Laurence)
   Deterring the drinking driver.

   Bibliography: p.
   Includes index.
   1. Drunk driving. 2. Drinking and traffic accidents. I. Title.
   K4037.R67   1984   345'.0247   84–5767
   ISBN 0–669–08717–3 (alk. paper)   342.5247
   ISBN 0–669–08199–X (pbk.:alk. paper)

Revised and Updated Edition
Copyright © 1984 by D.C. Heath and Company

Published simultaneously in Canada

Printed in the United States of America

Casebound International Standard Book Number: 0–669–08717–3

Paperbound International Standard Book Number: 0–669–08199–x

Library of Congress Catalog Card Number: 84–5767

To Judie and Mark

Contents

List of Figures and Tables

Figures

Tables

Foreword

No simple solutions exist to the problems caused by the abusive use of alcohol in conjunction with motor vehicles. These problems have been found to be extremely serious in every part of the world in which they have been systematically investigated, including countries as diverse as Sweden, France, the United Kingdom, Australia, and the United States.

This situation has come about through the confluence of two cultural elements, one ancient and the other of more-recent origin (Haddon 1963). The use of alcohol has been an integral, often disruptive practice in civilization since antiquity. The use of the motor vehicle and other equipment that place large amounts of power literally at the fingertips of the individual is a relatively recent development. Life and limb were at less risk—and society in less danger—in the case of the man on horseback who had too much to drink than in the case of the similarly intoxicated operator of a motor vehicle.

Moreover, there are many varieties of both drinking and vehicle use. Thus, there are many, somewhat differing, aspects of the overall problem. For example, the chronically offending alcoholic poses different control problems than those presented by the so-called social drinker (see chapter 1). The roadhouse located so that its intoxicated patrons have little alternative to driving home by car poses different control problems than the campus pub from which students can walk to their dormitories. At least in the case of the chronic alcoholic, considerable evidence shows that it may be difficult, if not impossible, to deal adequately with his abuse of alcohol in the motor-vehicle context without also dealing with his abuse of it in other contexts. Thus, Waller (1967) found both that substantial percentages of men apprehended for motor-vehicle offenses (various specific traffic violations and alcohol- and nonalcohol-related crashes) were known to community-service agencies because of an incident or problem related to the use of alcohol and that these percentages were far in excess of those of men with no violations or crashes. In contrast, whether the social drinker's sometime abuse of alcohol in relation to motor vehicles can be controlled separately from dealing with his use of alcohol in other contexts is presently unknown.

Contrary to common opinion, the overwhelming bulk of motor-vehicle crashes in which alcohol plays a role neither involves merely one or two drinks—far greater quantities of alcohol are involved—nor can the blood-alcohol concentrations defining driving while intoxicated in the statutes of the several states be reached by the ingestion of one or two drinks (Coldwell 1957). Lacking knowledge of this, some of the public apparently tends to believe that many of the people in alcohol-related offenses typically are moderate drinkers like most of themselves—"There but for the grace of God go I." They therefore believe it is unreasonable to penalize offenders unduly. These beliefs probably are reinforced by the fact that a majority of adult Americans do in fact sometimes drive after some drinking (U.S. House of Representatives 1968, chapter 4). Again, however, most people apparently do not appreciate the fact that those involved in crashes after drinking typically have consumed exceptionally large amounts of alcohol.

Popular awareness that alcohol abuse leads to motor-vehicle crashes was well established by the 1920s and 1930s. However, the emphasis, for example, in cartoons and fiction (Smith 1926), was less on the tragedy involved than on the supposed humor of such situations, a view that has continued to some extent even to the present. At the same time, the small scientific community concerned with the issues was unraveling the physiology of alcohol; its metabolism; the relationships between the amounts present in the blood, brain, and other tissues; and the means by which it could be measured, for example, in the breath of those who had been using it (Harger and Hulpieu 1956).

Having described the basic behavior and effects of alcohol in the body, research workers, beginning in 1938, increasingly turned their attention to quantifying the real-world effects of alcohol on motor-vehicle operation. By the early 1960s, the outlines and many of the specific details of the role of excessive alcohol use as a cause of motor-vehicle crashes were well established. These findings, which repeatedly have been confirmed, are of several types and are discussed in chapter 1 (see also Holcomb 1938; Smith and Popham 1951; Bjerver, Goldberg, and Linda 1955; Goldberg 1955; Lucas et al. 1955; Haddon and Bradess 1959; Haddon et al. 1961; McCarroll and Haddon 1962; Borkenstein et al. 1964; Haddon, Suchman, and Klein 1964; U.S. House of Representatives 1968; Hurst 1970; Jones and Joscelyn 1978; Wolfe 1975).

1. Drivers who have substantial blood-alcohol concentrations more often are responsible for the crashes in which they are involved than the other drivers. Their likelihood of being in crashes and their likelihood of responsibility for the crashes increase disproportionately the higher their blood-alcohol concentrations.

2. Crashes in which alcohol plays a role tend to be much more severe than other crashes. The more severe the crashes considered, the higher the percentages in which alcohol contributes. Thus, typically, in the United States, alcohol plays a role in less than 10 percent of run-of-the-mill crashes, about 20 percent of crashes involving serious injury to a driver or passenger, about 50 percent of all fatal crashes, and about 60 percent of all single-vehicle fatal crashes.

3. The overwhelming majority of drivers involved in serious and fatal crashes to which their own ingestion of alcohol contributed has blood-alcohol concentrations of 0.10 percent or higher, usually much higher. In addition, some such crash-involved drivers have concentrations in the range between 0.05 and 0.10.

4. On the average, some 90 percent of drivers operating vehicles in the United States have not been drinking to any measurable extent—that is, their blood-alcohol concentrations are zero. At least an additional 5 percent have blood-alcohol concentrations that, although measurable, are in the low range, between zero and 0.05 percent. These percentages are in sharp contrast to those cited in the preceding paragraphs from the examination of drivers in serious and fatal crashes to which alcohol has contributed.

5. Individuals arrested for drunken driving or hospitalized for motor-vehicle-crash injuries are far from a representative sample of the general population. The more alcohol is used by specific groups in that population, the far greater is their overrepresentation. For example, in Sweden, the heaviest and presumably most tolerant users of alcohol accounted for 45 percent of the alcohol-involved crashes despite their comprising only 9 percent of the general population.

6. Adult pedestrians fatally injured by motor vehicles also have substantially elevated blood-alcohol concentrations far more often than other adult pedestrians using the sidewalks and streets at the same time. Alcohol plays a role in about one-third of such deaths in the United States.

7. Although large amounts of alcohol must be ingested for blood-alcohol concentrations to reach or exceed 0.10 percent, roadside surveys in the United States have found that on weekend nights as many as 10 percent of all drivers have such illegal blood-alcohol concentrations.

As the scientific underpinnings of this field were increasingly established (National Safety Council 1978), Indiana became the first state to enact a motor-vehicle statute incorporating a specific blood-alcohol concentration (Indiana Acts 1939, chapter 48, §52). Enactment of similar laws by other states followed, and by the end of 1963, thirty-nine states and the District of Columbia had incorporated such provisions. The overwhelming majority of the statutes sets the relevant blood-alcohol concentrations at a very high 0.15 percent (U.S. House of Representatives 1968, chapter 7).

In the United States, controlling the alcohol-impaired driver traditionally has been a state function. However, the magnitude of the problem prompted federal action as early as the mid-1960s. In late 1966 and early 1967, officials of the then National Highway Safety Bureau (now the National Highway Traffic Safety Administration) met with representatives of all of the state governors to discuss the substance of the federal standards for state and local highway-safety programs called for under the Highway Safety Act of 1966 (23 U.S.C. 401 Supp. V, 1970). The federal standard, "Alcohol in Relation to Highway Safety," which was issued shortly thereafter, reflected these discussions and the need for bringing state laws into greater conformity both with each other and with the scientific evidence cited previously. Consequently, the federal standard, the first to deal with this subject, included among its provisions that "there . . . [be] a

specification by . . . [each] State . . . with respect to alcohol-related offenses . . . [of] the blood alcohol concentration not higher than 0.10 percent
by weight, which defines the terms *intoxicated* or *under the influence of
alcohol*" (U.S. House of Representatives 1967).

This standard and some public concern had, by 1971, induced all of the
states to adopt laws incorporating specific blood-alcohol concentrations.
Also, many states had lowered their statutorily specified concentrations to
at least 0.10 percent. It was not, however, until 1981 that every state had
adopted a 0.10 or lower value for a motor-vehicle-code violation.

Although the problem of alcohol-caused crashes had been well known
for some four decades, and although many legal and other efforts had been
made to control it, it was only with the work of Barmack and Payne,
reported in 1961, that anyone applied competent scientific methods to find
out whether any control program was in fact effective (see also Haddon,
Suchman, and Klein 1964). This was followed, beginning in the late 1960s
and early 1970s, by a series of competent scientific examinations of the efficacy of a variety of measures designed to reduce the problem of motor-
vehicle crashes initiated by the abuse of alcohol. This work has continued to
the present.

The continuing magnitude of the problem prompted the federal government to organize a major, nationwide program of Alcohol Safety Action
Projects (ASAPs) in the early 1970s. This program provided $78 million in
federal funds to thirty-five individual ASAPs in communities around the
country. It was intended to demonstrate the feasibility and practicality of a
systems approach—that is, one that is comprehensive and considers the in-
terrelationships of all aspects of the problem—and to demonstrate that
such an approach to the problem could save lives. Controversy surrounded
the evaluations of the ASAP program, and despite large increases in relevant activities (for example, in arrests and processing by the courts), there
was no substantial effect on fatal crashes, in particular, nighttime fatal
crashes (Zador 1976; Johnson, Levy, and Voas 1976; Zador 1977).

As noted in chapter 7, the scientific work of the past six decades on the
many aspects of the abuse of alcohol in relation to motor-vehicle crashes
often has been of very high quality and has established a large, interrelated
body of competent evidence on the subject. This is remarkable considering
the exceptional difficulties the individuals involved often have faced. The
subject matter and those who have worked on it usually have been held in
low regard in the scientific and academic pecking order. Persons active in
the field commonly have had to work with extremely limited resources, in
many cases borrowed from unrelated sources. In addition, perhaps the most
serious impediment has been that posed by the many who supposedly just
know which programs work, a situation with occasional parallels in relation
to the development and evaluation of treatments for cancer and some other

medical problems. Tragically, this intuitional approach repeatedly has blocked the very research needed to determine the actual effectiveness of specific control measures and how they might be improved; when that research has been done, its results commonly have found that the intuition was wrong.

Furthermore, it often has been impossible to answer certain critically important research questions such as those related to the effects of different sentences for offending drivers because assigning different jail terms and other penalties according to experimental requirements without violating fundamental American attitudes of fairness usually is not possible. In addition, the use and abuse of alcohol in relation to motor vehicles do not occur in a vacuum; they involve a welter of powerful and often conflicting economic, political, religious, and other interests that must be considered carefully by both research workers and those dealing with the problem from almost any standpoint. Nevertheless, as Ross extensively documents, the research to date has led to a number of clear-cut conclusions, for example:

> [C]hanges in the law promising increased certainty or combined certainty and severity of punishment reduce the amount of drinking and driving. . . . [but] changes in behavior resulting from changes in the certainty of threat, on the order of those achieved by policy innovations to date, are evanescent. . . .
>
> Innovations confined to manipulations of the severity of the legal punishment, without a concomitant change in its certainty, produce no effect on the apparent incidence of drinking and driving or its aftermath in crashes. . . . Virtually no evidence illustrates one way or the other, the effect of celerity. [pp. 102-104]

As a result, Ross believes that a promising approach would be one in which the apprehension of impaired drivers was substantially increased and in which penalties were imposed more swiftly and more certainly rather than more severely. However, such measures also would have to be carefully evaluated to determine if this in fact did produce the desired result.

In addition, excellent research has shown that lowering the minimum drinking age substantially increases fatal crashes involving teenagers (Williams et al. 1975) and that raising the minimum drinking age correspondingly decreases such crashes (Wagenaar and Douglass 1980; Insurance Institute for Highway Safety 1981(a); Williams et al. 1982).

With respect to another control measure—rehabilitation programs—the best research to date has found that drivers convicted of alcohol-related offenses have fewer crashes after their licenses have been suspended or revoked than after being sent through present types of rehabilitation (Preusser, Ulmer, and Adams 1976; Hagen, Williams, and McConnell 1979). However, since rehabilitation programs are evolving as new knowledge is acquired, the final word on their relative efficacy is by no means yet in. In addition, the effects of various combinations of suspensions (and revocations) used together with various types of treatment and rehabilitation need to be competently determined. Again, it is crucially important, insofar as possible, to base control policies on the best available scientific evidence rather than on guesswork or wishful thinking.

One does not, however, need scientific research or exhaustive familiarity with our society's present responses to the detection and processing of intoxicated drivers to know many reasons why the present system hardly could be expected to control the problems involved. To begin with, the chance that an intoxicated driver will be apprehended during his trip is extremely small—estimates place the likelihood at only one chance in hundreds, if not thousands, of such trips (Joscelyn and Jones 1971). In fact, one study has found that the police officer on street duty on the average arrests fewer than two intoxicated drivers a year from among the many thousands that must pass him (Fennessy et al. 1968).

Even when apprehended, only a tiny percentage of such drivers ever receive more than a slap on the wrist, even though severe legal sanctions are available under the laws of all the states. The system is riddled with escape hatches of bewildering ingeniousness, variety, and effectiveness. It is also replete with long delays that not only leave the offending driver free for long periods to continue to operate his vehicle but also separate so widely the disposition of his case from the date of his offense and his concomitant intoxication that the likelihood of conviction is even further reduced.

Fundamentally, these problems with the present system reflect the long-standing absence throughout the United States of any substantial public constituency effectively concerned with these problems and determined to make certain that they are thoroughly corrected. There are, however, indications that this tragic imbalance between the problem and the pressures for its correction may be beginning to improve. One should not infer, however, that the matter now is worse than formerly, since a great deal of solid evidence shows that it has been of similarly tragic magnitude for decades (U.S. House of Representatives 1968; Jones and Joscelyn 1978).

Nonetheless, the media appear to be paying somewhat more attention to identifying and publicizing at least some of the many hundreds of alcohol-initiated crashes occurring daily. More Americans seem to be concerned with the problem. Citizen groups determined to deal with it are increasingly being formed. In addition, some signs indicate that courts may be more willing than heretofore to apply the severe penalties that have long been available.

The substantial intractability of the problem should in no way impede strenuous efforts to find approaches that would help to reduce it. The fatal and other injuries and other damage caused by the alcohol-impaired driver also should not be written off. It is crucially important that the principal reason for concern with the problems of this field is not the tragic relationship between alcohol and highway crashes as such but rather the deaths, injuries, damage to property, and economic waste it produces. Since a number of practical, readily available measures can greatly reduce, although not eliminate, these human and other results of alcohol abuse in the highway context, the substantial intractability of at least portions of the overall problem pleads for energetic implementation of these preventive and ameliorative measures.

For example, many thousands of Americans die each year in crashes, in many of which other drivers are responsible, simply because the vehicles in which they were riding were not sufficiently well designed or constructed to protect them properly. For the same reason, hundreds of thousands of other people are injured needlessly or far more severely than would otherwise be the case. Despite the fact that antilacerative windshields have been on thousands of cars in Europe for years, they cannot be purchased today even as an option in the United States (Saint Gobain Vitrage 1980-1981; Insurance Institute for Highway Safety 1981b). The federal agency responsible for setting minimum vehicle-safety standards does not yet permit, let alone require, their use. Automatic-crash cushions (air bags), despite their availability on some cars in Europe, are neither required nor available for purchase in the United States (Sloyan 1981). Yet, the scientific evidence is clear that their presence in U.S. vehicles would reduce the severity of injuries in frontal crashes by some 65 percent (Mohan et al. 1976; Haddon 1980). Doors and side and rear windows are so poorly designed and constructed that about one-third of the occupants killed in single-vehicle crashes are ejected from the very vehicles that should contain and protect them (Insurance Institute for Highway Safety 1982).

The highway environment is full of built-in hazards that also needlessly increase the nation's totals of killed and maimed. Consider, in illustration, the millions of telephone and other poles placed closely along roadsides where they convert thousands of otherwise minor off-the-road mishaps into sentences of severe injury and death—a situation that would not be tolerated for a day along commercial and private airport runways (Insurance Institute for Highway Safety 1973; Fitzpatrick et al. 1974).

In sum, in addition to pursuing effective means for reducing the role of alcohol in highway crashes, it is essential to implement the many other measures that could contribute greatly and complementarily to reducing the carnage on U.S. roads (Haddon 1980; Haddon and Baker 1981).

In this excellent book, Ross has presented and examined the best research and data now available on the extent to which various control programs have succeeded in reducing crashes in which alcohol has played a role. He has considered the evidence, not only from the United States but also from other countries in which competent research workers have dealt with this issue. In doing so, he has significantly advanced a field of great public importance, suggested many of the directions subsequent work should take, and provided an invaluable resource and foundation for everyone concerned with this field specifically and with the overall deterrence of socially undesirable behavior.

Obviously, much can be done to reduce greatly the wasting of lives and property that has for years been accepted on the roads of the world. Public officials and others seeking to accomplish this objective should not postpone action pending the millenium of perfect scientific knowledge as to what works and what does not work. Rather, they must do the reasonable, using the best, if imperfect, information available, augmenting and modifying their efforts as better information is gained.

> *William Haddon, Jr., M.D.*
> President,
> Insurance Institute for
>   Highway Safety
> *Murray Blumenthal*
> Professor of Law,
> University of Denver

References

Barmack, J.E., and D.E. Payne. 1961. "The Lackland Accident Countermeasure Experiment." *Highway Research Board Proceedings* 40:513-522.

Bjerver, K.B.; L. Goldberg; and P. Linda. 1955. "Blood Alcohol Levels in Hospitalized Victims of Traffic Accidents." In *Proceedings of the Second International Conference on Alcohol and Road Traffic.* Toronto: Garden City Press Cooperative, pp. 92-102.

Borkenstein, R.F.; R.F. Crowther; R.P. Shumate; W.B. Ziel; R. Zylman; and A. Dale, eds. 1964. *The Role of the Drinking Driver in Traffic Accidents.* Bloomington, Indiana: Department of Police Administration, Indiana University.

Coldwell, B.B., ed. 1957. "Report on Impaired Driving Tests." Ottawa: Queen's Printer and Controller of Stationery.

Fennessy, E.F., Jr.; R.F. Borkenstein; H.C. Joksch; F.J. Leahy, Jr.; and K.B. Joscelyn. 1968. *The Technical Content of State and Community Police Traffic Services Programs.* Hartford, Conn.: Travelers Research Center.

Fitzpatrick, J.F., M.N. Sohn; T.E. Silfen; and R.H. Wood. 1974. *The Law and Roadside Hazards.* Charlottesville, Va.: The Michie Company.

Goldberg, L. 1955. "Drunken Drivers in Sweden." *Proceedings of the Second International Conference on Alcohol and Road Traffic*, pp. 112-127. Toronto: Garden City Press Cooperative.

Haddon, W. Jr. 1963. "Alcohol and Highway Accidents." *Proceedings of the Third International Conference on Alcohol and Road Traffic*, pp. 3-13. London.

_____.1980. "Options for the Prevention of Motor Vehicle Crash Injury. Keynote Address: Conference on Options for Prevention of Motor Vehicle Injury." *Israel Journal of Medical Sciences* 16:45-68.

Haddon, W., Jr., and V.A. Bradess. 1959. "Alcohol in the Single Vehicle Fatal Accident: Experience of Westchester County, New York." *Journal of the American Medical Association* 169:1587-1593.

Haddon, W., Jr.; P. Valien; J.R. McCarroll; and C.J. Umberger. 1961. "A Controlled Investigation of the Characteristics of Adult Pedestrians Fatally Injured by Motor Vehicles in Manhattan." *Journal of Chronic Diseases* 14:655-678.

Haddon, W. Jr.,E.A. Suchman; and D. Klein. 1964. *Accident Research: Methods and Approaches*. New York: Harper & Row.

Haddon, W., Jr., and S.P. Baker. 1981. "Injury Control." In *Preventive and Community Medicine*, edited by D.W. Clark and B. MacMahon, pp. 109-140. Boston: Little, Brown & Company.

Hagen, R.E.; R.L. Williams; and E.J. McConnell. 1979. "The Traffic Safety Impact of Alcohol Abuse Treatment as an Alternative to Mandated Licensing Controls." *Accident Analysis and Prevention* 11:275-291.

Harger, R.N., and H.R. Hulpieu. 1956. "The Pharmacology of Alcohol." In *Alcoholism*, edited by G.N. Thompson, pp. 103-232. Springfield, Ill.: Charles C Thomas.

Holcomb, R.L. 1938. "Alcohol in Relation to Traffic Accidents." *Journal of the American Medical Association* 3:1076-1085.

Hurst, P.M. 1970. "Estimating the Effectiveness of Blood Alcohol Limits." *Behavioral Research in Highway Safety* 1:87-99.

Insurance Institute for Highway Safety. 1973. "Boobytrap!" 16 mm color sound film. Washington, D.C.

_____. 1981a. "Raising Drinking Age Reduces Fatal Crashes." *Status Report* 16:10.

_____. 1981b. "Faces in Crashes." 16 and 35 mm color sound film. Washington, D.C.

_____. 1982. *Status Report* 17:1.

Johnson, P.; P. Levy; and R. Voas. 1976. "A Critique of the Paper Statistical Evaluation of the Effectiveness of Alcohol Safety Action Projects'." *Accident Analysis and Prevention* 8:67-77.

Jones, R.K., and K.B. Joscelyn. 1978. "Alcohol and Highway Safety 1978: A Review of the State of Knowledge." Ann Arbor: Michigan Highway Safety Research Institute, UM HSRI 78 9.

Joscelyn, K.B., and R.K. Jones. 1971. *A Systems Approach to the Analysis of the Drinking Driver Control System.* Bloomington: Institute for Research in Public Safety, Indiana University.

Lucas, G.H.; W. Kalow; J.D. McColl; B.A. Griffith; and H.W. Smith. 1955. "Quantitative Studies of the Relationship between Alcohol Levels and Motor Vehicle Accidents." *Proceedings of the Second International Conference on Alcohol and Road Traffic,* pp. 139-142. Toronto: Garden City Press Cooperative.

McCarroll, J.R.; and W. Haddon, Jr. 1962. "A Controlled Study of Fatal Automobile Accidents in New York City." *Journal of Chronic Diseases* 15:811-826.

Mohan, D.; P.L. Zador; B. O'Neill; and M. Ginsburg. 1976. "Air Bags and Lap/Shoulder Belts—A Comparison of Their Effectiveness in Real World, Frontal Crashes." *Proceedings of the Twentieth Conference of the American Association for Automotive Medicine,* pp. 315-335. Morton Grove, Ill.

National Safety Council. 1978. *Recommendations of the Committee on Alcohol and Drugs, 1936-1977.* Chicago.

Preusser, D.F.; R.G. Ulmer; J.R. Adams. 1976. "Driver Record Evaluation of a Drinking Driver Rehabilitation Program." *Journal of Safety Research* 8:98-105.

Saint Gobain Vitrage. 1980-1981. Submissions to the following National Highway Traffic Safety Administration dockets: No. 009 (12 June 1980); No. 001 (Supplement of 26 September 1980); No. 035 (Supplement of 22 April 1981); No. 035A (Supplement of 2 July 1981); No. 039 (Supplement of 17 August 1981).

Sloyan, Patrick J. "The Air Bag Lives—Abroad." *Newsday,* 9 November 1981, part III, p. 3.

Smith, H.W., and R.E. Popham. 1951. "Accident Contribution of Drivers as a Function of Their Blood Alcohol Levels." *Proceedings of the First International Conference on Alcohol and Traffic,* pp. 150-151. Stockholm: Kugelbergs Boktryckeri.

Smith, T. 1926. *Topper: An Improbable Adventure.* New York: McBride.

U.S. House of Representatives, Committee on Public Works. 1967. *Highway Safety Program Standards.* Report from the Secretary of Transportation to the Congress, as required by the Highway Safety Act of 1966, print no. 7 (Washington: U.S. Government Printing Office).

_____ . 1968. *1968 Alcohol and Highway Safety Report.* Report from the Secretary of Transportation to the Congress, in accordance with the requirements of section 204 of the Highway Safety Act of 1966, print no. 90-34 (Washington: U.S. Government Printing Office).

Wagenaar, A.C., and R.L. Douglass. 1980. *An Evaluation of the Changes in the Legal Drinking Ages in Michigan.* Ann Arbor: Highway Safety Research Institute, University of Michigan, UM HSRI 78 9.

Waller, J.A. 1967. "Identification of Problem Drinkers among Drunken Drivers." *Journal of the American Medical Association.* 200:124-130.

Williams, A.F.; R.F. Rich; P.L. Zador; and L.S. Robertson. 1975. "The Legal Minimum Drinking Age and Fatal Motor Vehicle Crashes." *Journal of Legal Studies* 4:219-239.

Williams, A.F.; P.L. Zador; S.S. Harris; and R.S. Karpf. 1982. "The Effect of Raising the Legal Minimum Drinking Age on Fatal Crash Involvement." *Journal of Legal Studies,* in press.

Wolfe, A.C. 1975. *Characteristics of Alcohol-Impaired Drivers.* Warrendale, Pa.: Society of Automotive Engineers 750878.

Zador, P.L. 1976. "Statistical Evaluation of the Effectiveness of 'Alcohol Safety Action Projects'." *Accident Analysis and Prevention* 8:51-66.

_____ . 1977. "A Rejoinder to a Critique of the Paper 'Statistical Evaluation of the Effectiveness of Alcohol Safety Action Projects' by Johnson et al." *Accident Analysis and Prevention* 9:15-19.

Preface to the
Revised Edition

The genuine intellectual must be the "enemy of the people" who tells the world things it either does not want to hear or cannot understand.
                                                    —Henry Morgenthau

The problem of drunk driving occupies an important place in the intersection of social science and social policy in contemporary America. The attempt to control the problem has produced a flood of legislation. In 1982, for example, 378 bills relating to drunk driving were introduced in 37 states, and 38 of these became law in 25 states. Many of the new laws embodied provisions for social scientific evaluation. Social scientists on their own have seized the opportunity provided by these numerous "natural experiments" to explore the capabilities and limitations of law for guiding and controlling behavior. The social scientists' findings are being made into policy, providing the basis for critical appraisals of what has been done and guidance for future efforts.

Because of this scholarly and political ferment, *Deterring the Drinking Driver* has had the good fortune to attract attention beyond that usually accorded to academic monographs. The publishers have authorized this paperback edition to permit the wider circulation of the book among both social scientists and people working in public policy. I hope particularly to extend the readership of this book to university students and citizen activists in the movement to control drunk driving. The significance of this work for these two audiences will be discussed here.

For social scientists, this book is offered both as a review of what is known concerning the newly recognized problem of drunk driving and as a report on attempts to cope with the problematical behavior through law—specifically the criminal justice system. It marshals the available evidence concerning the validity of a currently popular theoretical paradigm—deterrence—and indicates through this evidence the strengths and weaknesses of the paradigm as a description and explanation of behavior subjected to legal control.

Beyond this use, the student of social science will find here a possible model of how to investigate and present information on the state of knowledge relating to a given topic. The task of reviewing the state of knowledge is an important recurring problem in scientific work. It serves to establish the point of departure from which new investigations can originate, and to indicate the most fruitful directions for these new investigations. The student finds a need for such a review when preparing a term paper, thesis or dissertation; the professional finds the need when endeavoring to convince funders of the importance of proposed research or to convince journal editors of the importance of reporting the results of completed research.

My personal experience as a grant program administrator—director of the Program in Law and Social Sciences at the National Science Foundation—and as the editor of a journal, the *Law and Policy Quarterly*, has taught me the importance of competent, theoretically oriented reviews of the literature. The successful proposal or manuscript invariably involves establishing the state of existing knowledge and demonstrating that what is proposed or has been accomplished serves to advance knowledge in the field. Of course, the successful proposal or manuscript is also able to demonstrate that the specific methods proposed or utilized can support the conclusions advanced. This latter task lies in the area of methodology, which is generally well taught in our universities. But the former task is less frequently addressed and mastered in training. I have seen many elaborate proposals and methodologically sophisticated research reports rejected by review panels because the author had not convinced them that the prospective or achieved results added anything significant to the field of inquiry. What is worth doing is worth doing well, but is it worth doing in the first place? This question may be answered by following the model offered here.

This book is organized around specific predictions or hypotheses flowing from the deterrence proposition, which states that threatened behavior will be inhibited to the extent that the punishment is perceived to be swift, certain, and severe. The intuitive plausibility of deterrence and the predictive success of allied models in the area of market behavior compensate somewhat for the deficiency of the proposition as theory, to wit, its isolated intellectual status. Unlike the best scientific theory, deterrence is not well integrated into a larger body of principles capable of explaining broad ranges of facts. For this reason I speak of the deterrence "proposition" rather than deterrence "theory." Moreover, the most direct empirical reference of deterrence is to subjective states, perceptions, and expectations, rather than to more easily measured external behavior. Most tests of the proposition are therefore indirect and inferential. However, the deterrence proposition is able to organize the diverse materials presented here in a much more detailed fashion than other current theoretical ideas. Such an organization brings together experiences from many countries, analyzed by divergent and often defective research methods. It reveals parallels in results, increasing confidence in interpretations which, in isolation, seem highly speculative. For instance, it shows that the decline in effectiveness of new drunk-driving laws reflects public consciousness of low probabilities of punishment. It also points to gaps in knowledge and suggests priorities for the application of limited research resources. For instance, it shows the need to search for and evaluate drunk-driving countermeasures based on swiftness of punishment.

Whereas this book suggests the location of fruitful research opportunities to the social scientist, it suggests the nature of promising drunk-driving countermeasures to the citizen activist. It documents the promise and limitations of deterrence-based measures, which seem to "work" in the short run but not over time. My conclusion is that the main limitation of attempts to deter drunk driving lies in the failure of all jurisdictions to date to raise the actual risk of punishment to a level that cannot be overlooked by potential violators. In this framework, many currently proposed countermeasures seem to be well-conceived. Examples are increasing the number of breath tests of drivers during nighttime hours, basing convictions on the results of these tests, and using administrative rather than criminal procedures to secure swift and certain punishment of offenders. However, many currently proposed countermeasures, especially those mandating unusually severe punishment of routine offenders, seem misguided in the light of my analysis. Experience suggests that these measures are more suitable as retributive than as deterrent policies. They may make victims feel better but they do not prevent future drunk driving.

The deterrence proposition may fail as a guide to policy not because it is scientifically invalid but, at least in part, because it is so hard to apply in the real world of police, prosecutors, judges, and juries. These criminal-justice system personnel often fail to apprehend, prosecute, and convict offenders in numbers large enough that deterrence-based expectations have a reasonable chance of fulfillment. This interpretation is supported by parallels in the experience of apparent successes and failures of deterrence-oriented measures in areas other than drunk driving. Where threatened behavior occurs in public view and where a large proportion of violators is punished, deterrent policy appears to be successful. Intensive patrol and high fines have almost eliminated illegal parkers on midtown Manhattan streets, for example. In contrast, where the violations are massive and the control effort is relatively insignificant, deterrence-based measures appear to be inadequate. One illustration can be found in the fact that the Internal Revenue Service loses an estimated $80 to 100 billion every year to tax cheaters, despite its computer-based enforcement resources.

I do not mean to discourage the citizen activists who have discovered the drunk-driving problem in the 1980s. I wish to guide them in demanding policies that are not only intuitively appealing but that also have a reasonable probability of producing significant reductions in deaths and injuries due to alcohol-impaired driving. To be sure, there is hope for deterrence-based countermeasures for drunk driving: short-run savings of lives and injuries can be virtually guaranteed for well-publicized efforts aimed at increasing the likelihood of punishment for violators. Long-range effects may be within reach, though at a price that the public may pay only grudgingly. However, the limitations of these measures should be squarely faced. Alternatives based on other conceptualizations of the problem should be considered along with, if not necessarily instead of, deterrence-based policies. Subsidized public transportation to and from drinking establishments, license curfews and restrictions on drinking for young people, and designing vehicles that produce less injury in crashes may not punish the drunk driver, but they can reduce the toll of injuries and lives lost due to drunk driving.

These alternative strategies, being nonpunitive, may fail to appeal to those who define the drunk driver as a villain, but if prevention of future harm is more important than retribution for past injuries, they should be adopted. Most people killed by drunk drivers are in fact themselves either drunk drivers, drunk passengers, or drunk pedestrians; many effective countermeasures will therefore benefit the very people who may be felt to deserve punishment. To the extent that such countermeasures are nonetheless efficient and effective means of preventing deaths and injuries, I hope that citizen activists motivated by personal losses will heed Donne's admonition: "Every man's death diminishes me, for I am of mankind. . . ."

1 The Problem of Drinking and Driving

In terms of the magnitude of its effect on the structure and functioning of the societies in which it has become embedded, the automobile is surely one of the most crucial inventions of human history. It has changed the physical and social dimensions of human existence by modifying the preexisting bases of everyday life. It has created the conditions for an economic and cultural life of incredible richness for masses of people. It has also opened a Pandora's box of associated costs including the tragic accumulation of crash injuries and deaths.

The contribution of alcohol to traffic crashes has been recognized by experts for several decades, indeed for as long as the automobile has been considered serious transportation rather than a rich man's toy (T. Cameron 1977, p. 123). The nature and extent of this contribution was initially only vaguely understood, and both popular and legal views of the problem centered on the grossly intoxicated driver, the so-called killer drunk (Gusfield 1981). In response to this image, laws were promulgated that prohibited driving in an "intoxicated condition," driving while "under the influence of intoxicating liquor," or just plain "drunk driving" (Fisher and Reeder 1974, p. 173). These laws, which I term *classical*, aimed their proscriptions at clearly blameworthy conduct. Penalties and procedures were drawn from the general criminal law and seemed to be appropriate to the behavior in question.

Research Traditions

The inadequacy of the killer-drunk image of the relationship between alcohol and crashes became apparent as technology began to permit quantitative analyses of alcohol in the blood. This technology developed about the time of World War I and led to two major lines of research—one, focusing on the relationship between blood-alcohol concentrations, skills, and judgment in experimental and limited field settings; and the second, on the relative crash risk associated with various blood-alcohol concentrations among drivers actually on the highways.

The first line of research has included laboratory studies of experimentally induced blood-alcohol concentrations on performance of skills expected to be related to driving; for example, errors in performance on

1

machinery simulating the driving task and errors observed in driving on closed experimental courses. (The blood-alcohol concentrations studied have been far lower than those that would have produced clinically evident drunkenness.) As summarized in one recent review, the laboratory studies have shown that, although performance of simple tasks does not deteriorate markedly with low blood-alcohol concentrations, more-difficult tasks (especially tasks that require divided attention like driving) are noticeably affected (Christensen, Fosser, and Glad 1978). This finding has been confirmed in simulator and closed-course studies, which frequently have found marked deterioration at blood-alcohol concentrations between 0.05 and 0.08 percent (unit of weight/percentage of volume). These concentrations are of the order that could be ᴜbtained by a 150-pound person's consuming three to five ounces of liquor within a short period of time, hardly the picture inherent in the stereotypical characterization of the drunk driver. (The blood-alcohol concentration resulting from consumption of a given number of drinks varies with the weight of the individual, rate of drinking, presence or absence of food in the stomach, and type of drink and concentration of alcohol in it, among other factors.)

The second line of research—comparing blood-alcohol concentrations of drivers experiencing crashes with those of non-crash-involved drivers—has led to the conclusion that alcohol is disproportionately found in the blood of people in crashes compared to people not in crashes. Alternatively stated, a considerably higher risk of crash involvement exists on the part of drinking drivers (Jones and Joscelyn 1978, pp. 7-34). In the more-serious crashes, especially single-vehicle fatal crashes, over half of the drivers have blood-alcohol concentrations greater than 0.10 percent, and almost three-quarters of these drivers have concentrations greater than 0.15 percent.

The major achievements in this line of research are summarized in figure 1-1, which reproduces calculations by Paul Hurst (1970) concerning the relative probabilities of crash involvement at different blood-alcohol concentrations. The figure, based on five North American studies conducted between the 1930s and the 1960s, shows that concentrations of alcohol greater than 0.05 percent in the blood are associated with important increases in crash probabilities. Relative crash probabilities increase exponentially.

These findings have been confirmed by the results of more-recent studies (for example, Farris, Malone, and Lilliefors 1976; Boston University School of Law 1976). Apart from the Manhattan study, which was based on a very small sample, the literature has found that the increased probability of crash involvement is even greater for crashes involving fatal and serious injuries and for drivers judged responsible for crashes, including drivers in single-car crashes. Furthermore, as the severity of the crashes increases—

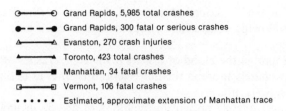

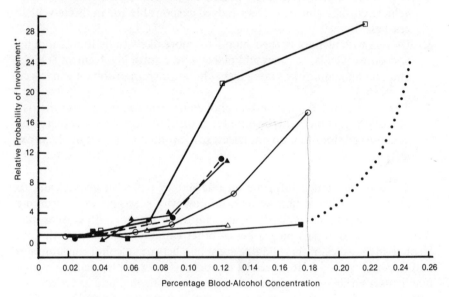

Source: Hurst 1970, p. 91. Reprinted with permission.
*1.0 = Relative probability at zero alcohol.

Figure 1-1. Relative Probability of Crash Involvement as a Function of
Blood-Alcohol Concentration

that is, from property-damage crashes, to injury-producing crashes, to fatal
crashes, and finally to single-vehicle fatal crashes—the percentages of
drivers with positive blood-alcohol concentrations increase; average concentrations among the drivers with alcohol in their blood increase substantially.

The State of Knowledge

Voluminous literature now exists on the relationship between alcohol and
traffic crashes, summarized in recent reviews by students of alcoholism (T.

Cameron 1977) and of traffic safety (Jones and Joscelyn 1978). These reviews point to the following conclusions about alcohol and crashes:

1. Alcohol is often found in the blood of drivers involved in crashes of all kinds and proportionately more in the more-serious crashes as defined by fatalities and serious injuries.
2. Alcohol is disproportionately present in the blood of drivers in single-vehicle crashes and of drivers judged responsible for multiple-vehicle crashes.
3. Drivers with alcohol in their blood are more likely to be found at night and on weekends, at times and places where crash involvement is high, and among people like young men who are disproportionately involved in crashes.
4. The more elevated the blood-alcohol concentration, the greater the risk of a crash. It should also be noted that the risk is considerably increased at concentrations that do not necessarily produce clinical signs of intoxication.

There is also much information relevant to policy in general and to deterrence in particular that we do not know with precision about drinking drivers. For example, some of the association of alcohol with crashes may reflect the causal impact on crashes of other variables associated with both alcohol and crashes, rather than a causal link between alcohol consumption and crashes. Such variables could be social (for example, being a young man causes an increase in both consumption of alcohol and experience of crashes) or psychological (for example, being depressed causes both). One of the suggested alternative explanations of the alcohol-crash link is that both drinking and experiencing crashes relate to differential willingness to take risks. The risk-prone individual is likely to count among drivers with high blood-alcohol concentrations as well as among crash-involved drivers (for example, see Zylman 1974, 1975).

It is also unclear whether the same group of drivers that accumulates drinking-and-driving convictions gets involved in crashes, although both samples are characterized by heavy drinkers. Another point of contention is whether drivers who have become involved in fatal crashes form part of the same group as those involved in less-serious crashes. One of the major questions that has yet to be answered with precision concerns the role of alcoholics, or problem drinkers—as contrasted with social drinkers—in the various groups mentioned here.

In short, although the killer-drunk image is not supported by research, alcohol in the blood is known to be an important correlate of traffic crashes, especially the most serious and damaging ones. The exact role of alcohol in this association is not fully understood, and not all of the association between elevated blood-alcohol concentrations and serious crashes is necessarily direct and causal:

> [A]lthough research has clearly indicated that alcohol plays a substantial role in traffic problems, both at the time of the accident and in the personal histories of accident-involved persons, any general, single-cause model of traffic accidents cannot account for the intricate interrelationships of personality, situational, and demographic factors in the chain of events which lead to traffic crashes. [T. Cameron 1977, p. 258].

However, a direct and causal link very likely explains a large part of the association between alcohol and crashes. Thus, from the policy viewpoint, techniques restraining people from drinking and driving are likely to have important social payoffs. One possible avenue for achieving this policy goal is deterrence through law.

2 The Deterrence Model

Functions of Criminal Law

Deterrence is but one of the intended functions of criminal law, and it needs to be placed in context. Other goals of this kind of law are retribution, incapacitation, and rehabilitation.

Retribution is the punishment function of criminal law. It depends on acknowledgment of the moral blameworthiness of engaging in prohibited behavior, and it repays such behavior with unpleasantness or pain in proportion to the deserts of the offender. Retribution is not directly related to social control; presumably the offender should be punished even though the punishment would have no further effect on the behavior of either the offender or anyone else, since evil deserves punishment. However, two links between retribution and social control have been noted in the literature. The functionalist tradition in sociology points to the possibility that punishing violators may strengthen a threatened norm and increase group cohesion in the face of deviance. Indeed, a certain level of punished deviance may be necessary and desirable in any group in order to provide illustrations of the normative boundaries for behavior (Erikson 1966). Furthermore, a strong claim can be made that the degree of blameworthiness of the offender sets limits on the nature and extent of the measures that can be applied to him by criminal law in order to achieve its purposes (Packer 1968). Even well-intentioned and humanitarian treatment, designed for and capable of improving the offender's future behavior and happiness, may not be applied to him against his will in the absence of prior blameworthy conduct.

A second function of criminal law is incapacitation of the offender. This is achieved through legal sanctions that restrict the offender's ability to commit new violations, even though he might wish to do so. Incapacitation operates on the unreformed offender and assumes no change in motivation associated with the previous crime. The classic example is imprisonment, which eliminates recidivism for a period of time by physically constraining the offender. The offender may, alternatively, remain free but in circumstances in which the opportunity to commit further offenses is restricted (the example of transportation of offenders to Australia comes to mind). In the case of driving offenses, less-restrictive alternatives for incapacitation are available, although these may act imperfectly. Examples include suspension or revocation of the driver's license and confiscation of vehicles owned or driven by the offender.

Rehabilitation refers to measures such as education and treatment that are applied to offenders in an attempt to change their motivation to commit further offenses. Rehabilitative measures normally are nonpunitive and easier for the twentieth-century conscience to support than other ways of dealing with criminals. However, the application of these measures in their usual form—independent of the wishes of the offender—requires a kind of retributive justification that distinguishes them from more-orthodox education and treatment. Moreover, the programs currently utilized for violators of traditional criminal laws seldom have been judged successful when evaluated by competent social-science research. This fact may well yield pessimism concerning prospects for rehabilitating drinking drivers, but legal workers in this area are strongly motivated and the pessimism may be premature. The state of the literature is summarized by Philip Cook:

> It is safe to conclude that correctional rehabilitation programs, taken collectively, have had a small effect on crime rates in the past, and that a number of notable programs have failed completely. But as long as it can be shown that one or more existing, practical rehabilitation strategies can produce a positive effect on convicts' behavior in the community, then rehabilitation remains a viable objective of the correctional system. [1977, p. 166]

General deterrence is yet another goal of the legal enterprise. For conceptual clarity, general deterrence must be distinguished from special or specific deterrence. General deterrence refers to the effect of threatened punishment upon the population in general, influencing potential violators to refrain from a prohibited act through a desire to avoid the legal consequences. The threat is both general and conditional; regardless of who you are, if you commit the violation you will be punished. General deterrence thus is expected to affect the behavior of all persons addressed, whether or not they have ever committed the offense in question. Specific deterrence refers to the effect of punishments experienced by convicted offenders in making them more sensitive to the consequences of the legal threat in their future activities. Specific deterrence thus is more closely related to rehabilitation than to general deterrence.

Scandinavian and German criminologists have further clarified the concept of general deterrence, or general prevention (Andenaes 1974; Hauge 1978). This concept subsumes both a short-term mechanism in which people react through fear of threat and long-term mechanisms in which habit formation and moral education follow from exposure of the population over time to the short-term threat. Thus, what is done at first due to fear of punishment later is done voluntarily due to internalization of the legal standards in question.

The mechanism to be discussed in the balance of this book is the short-term component of general deterrence, which has also been termed *simple deterrence.* This focus is not intended to deny the existence of the long-term components. However, their attainment is expected to be a function of the adequacy and persistence of the short-term threat, which thus becomes a prior concern. Moreover, policymakers adopting the deterrence approach to controlling drinking and driving have had in mind the simple deterrence model, which thus serves as a proper basis for evaluation of current policies. Finally, demonstration of the origins of nonlegal norms in the historical exposure of a population to specific legal threats is extremely hard to accomplish by scientifically persuasive techniques. I shall leave that task to other toilers in the sociolegal vineyard.

Simple Deterrence

Our understanding of simple deterrence has its origins in the speculations of Beccaria, Feuerbach, and the English utilitarians. It can be regarded as a restatement of the first law of demand in economics. Briefly, it proposes that the efficacy of a legal threat is a function of the perceived certainty, severity, and swiftness or celerity of punishment in the event of a violation of the law. The greater the perceived likelihood of apprehension, prosecution, conviction, and punishment, the more severe the perceived eventual penalty, and the more swiftly it is perceived to be administered, the greater will be the deterrent effect of the threat.

This model is intuitively plausible and is supported by its association with a basic law of economic theory that has received impressive confirmation over the years. Therefore, the question usually posed for the model is not whether it is valid in general but under what conditions it is more or less valid. As stated by the relevant panel of the National Academy of Sciences:

> [T]he evidence certainly favors a proposition supporting deterrence more than it favors one asserting that deterrence is absent. The major challenge for future research is to estimate the magnitude of the effects of different sanctions on various crime types. [Blumstein, Cohen, and Nagin 1978, p. 7]

In the past several years, social scientists have become increasingly interested in the deterrence issue conceived—as here—in terms of both its meaning for policy and its implications for understanding the role of law in social control. Several issues have been identified, in studies of traditional crimes, concerning the conditions for deterrent effectiveness (for example, Grasmick and Green 1980; Tittle 1980). For instance, to what degree are the three components of the model—certainty, severity, and celerity of punishment—interactive? Does severity of penalty, for example, make a difference only when relative certainty of apprehension and conviction exists? Do thresholds exist below which no effects can be expected? Do the components of the deterrence model interact with other social-control variables such as peer-group pressures and internalized standards of behavior? Is deterrence dependent on the social and psychological characteristics of the potential violator—age and sex, as well as attitude toward risk, future orientation, and so forth (see Chambliss 1966; Zimring and Hawkins 1973)? What is the relationship between actual certainty, severity, and celerity of punishment and the perceptual analogues of these variables that are involved in the deterrence model (see Gibbs 1975)?

This book addresses these questions with information derived from studies of drinking-and-driving laws. As compared with the literature based on studies of more-traditional crimes, the drinking-and-driving literature deals with offenses that are less anchored in morality and other nonlegal systems of rules, presenting the opportunity to study legal regulation in comparative isolation. Moreover, studies of the effects of drinking-and-driving laws are fortunate in finding relatively valid and reliable measures of these effects and a relatively broad range of legal innovations, the effects of which can be investigated by appropriate methods. The nature of these data and methods forms the next subject for discussion, prior to presenting the evidence provided by a survey of world literature.

3 Methods for Studying Deterrence

When a policymaker intervenes in the stream of social activity, how does he know what he has accomplished? How does he judge whether his intervention has produced desired consequences or, for that matter, feared or even unanticipated side effects? More broadly, how does the social-science analyst come to conclusions about the effects of social interventions? This chapter reviews some typical but fallible procedures used to study deterrence-based intervention and suggests a proper method for achieving valid conclusions in such enterprises.

The starting point for answering any question in a scientifically acceptable fashion is the occurrence of change in the observable world. Intervention is accomplished by varying the level of a measurable independent, or causal, variable. The effect of intervention can be known through measures of theoretically linked dependent, or effect, variables. The intervention may be regarded as accompanied by a theory that links a change in a hypothetically causal variable to changes in one or more associated effect variables. The crucial methodological issues are the validity of the measures in question and the ability to interpret the associated changes as confirming the intervention theory rather than resulting from plausible alternative explanations (see Campbell and Stanley 1963).

Measurement Issues

Traditional deterrence studies face considerable problems with both of these issues. The measurement issue is directly confronted in the form of the dark-figure problem—the large number of unknown crimes relative to those that are known. Crime in general, and in most of its specific categories, is very poorly measured. The sources of our usual statistics, police departments, are far removed from knowledge of criminal acts, since these must be both noted and reported to the police in a process distinguished for its lack of incentives (it takes time and effort, and little good is likely to come to the reporter) and presence of disincentives (shame, loss of face, even actual danger to the reporter). Thus, only a small and variable fraction of most criminal acts is officially known and available for study. Furthermore, this fraction may vary as a consequence of certain interventions, producing apparent changes that are actually due to variations in measurement but that can be erroneously interpreted as confirming a theory of intervention effects (this is the problem of "instrumentation" noted by Campbell and Stanley 1963). Although the dark figure of traditional crime can be reduced by devices such as surveying the public concerning their experiences of victimization, considerable bias and error still remain in survey-based data on traditional crimes because of errors in recall and interpretation on the part of the surveyed population.

Studies of the effects of drinking-and-driving-law interventions are favored by considerably better data than those available for studies of interventions in traditional criminal law. I am not referring to police reports of impaired drivers or arrest statistics, which are unreliable (Waller 1971) and also subject to dark figures exceeding 99 percent; rather, the link between blood-alcohol concentrations and serious crashes, documented in chapter 1, permits reliance on statistics of fatalities and serious injuries as surrogate measures for drinking and driving. These statistics routinely are gathered in considerable detail in many jurisdictions throughout the world and are available at little or no cost through official sources. Changes in these figures can, with some confidence, be relied on as indexing changes in drinking-and-driving behavior.

Fatalities and serious injuries have low dark figures because the need to treat injuries and to process cadavers brings virtually all cases to the attention of health and hospital authorities with well-developed statistical systems. Furthermore, data concerning crashes resulting in serious damage to life and limb, when reported to the police, are very likely treated less casually than those concerning relatively minor crashes.

Data concerning serious crashes do have limitations as bases for scientific evaluation of interventions in drinking-and-driving law. For one thing, although some refined data series (for example, single-vehicle crashes on weekend nights) have very substantial associations with drinking and driving, a large fraction of serious crashes is not alcohol related and cannot be expected to change as a function of successful laws [Moore and Gerstein (1981) estimate that a totally effective deterrent measure might reduce fatalities by no more than one-fourth]. Therefore, taken at face value, the data on serious crashes are likely to understate the effects of drinking-and-driving laws. For another thing, the more specific the series, the smaller the data bases and therefore the greater the random variability. This fact causes many series, especially those based on small jurisdictions, to appear "nervous" and variable and makes it more difficult to find statistical significance in changes associated with interventions.

Data on serious crashes have the advantage of general availability and access at little or no cost. A more-expensive but direct measure of drinking and driving comes from specially commissioned surveys of blood-alcohol concentrations among driving populations. Drivers are stopped at randomly selected survey points and asked to contribute breath samples for scientific analysis. These analyses form the basis of a considerable international literature although, because of the cost of this technique, it is rarely performed in an extensive time series (for an exception, see Noordzij 1977). Refusals, although surprisingly rare, can present a problem for these measures, especially when the measures are used as a basis for international comparisons.

A less-expensive measure than surveys—and more direct than fatality and injury statistics—is furnished by testing drivers in fatal crashes for blood alcohol, a procedure now routinely followed in many jurisdictions. However, the procedure is vulnerable to incompleteness, since testing must be done within a very short time of the crash to be meaningful, and it sometimes requires the cooperation of isolated independent physicians who may be less skillful or cooperative than hospital personnel. Furthermore, to the extent that the causation of fatal crashes is importantly different from that of other serious crashes (an open question, as noted in chapter 1), a considerable part of the problem addressed by the legal intervention is ignored.

In sum, three techniques are available for use in evaluating the deterrent effect of drinking-and-driving law that help to resolve some of the problems of measurement validity found in more-traditional deterrence research. Although these techniques differ in quality, in the directness of relationship to policy, and in their cost and accessibility, together they render measurement of deterrent impact considerably simpler and more valid than techniques more normally available. They help to increase the usefulness of studies of drinking-and-driving law for understanding the deterrence mechanism.

Problems of Causal Inference

When a change is found in valid measures of dependent, or effect, variables at the time of an intervention, the problem arises of ascribing this change to the intervention rather than to a variety of possible alternative rival explanations. In the typical example of adoption of a new law or inception of a crackdown on drinking and driving, four categories of rival explanatory hypotheses are particularly prominent: (1) "history," (2) "maturation," (3) "instability," and (4) "regression" (Campbell and Stanley 1963; Ross 1973).

To illustrate these problems, suppose that a new law promulgated in the state of Ruritania is associated with a decline in crash-related fatalities from 100 last year to 80 this year. The theoretical explanation for this decline of 20 deaths lies in the deterrent effect of the new law. The rival hypothesis of history refers to all other specific events that have taken place between the two years that might affect the occurrence of fatal crashes. Illustrations include the completion of a considerable stretch of limited-access superhighway (with low crash rates) in Ruritania or exceptionally favorable weather (rain, for instance, lowers the fatal-crash rate although it increases that for minor crashes). The category of history could also encompass different kinds of law, including one aimed at the installation of passive restraint devices for vehicle occupants. Maturation, in contrast, raises the possibility that the change was due to long-range trends in fatal crashes rather than to discrete events. Perhaps the population of Ruritania is newly introduced to the automobile and is learning better driving skills over time. Perhaps the proportion of young men (a group with high crash rates) in the driving population is diminishing over the years due to demographic changes. If factors like these produce steeply declining trends in casualties, they could possibly explain the observed decline of 20 deaths in Ruritania. Instability refers to the fact that all social data vary from time to time for a variety of reasons that, taken together, we call chance. Is the decline of 20 deaths of the magnitude that occurs relatively frequently in comparing two measures of this casualty variable? If so, we would not be able to rule out an explanation in terms of instability. Is the decline extraordinary? Then instability would be implausible. Finally, regression refers to the fact that when conditions are abnormal or extreme in any way, they have a tendency to look less extreme or more normal on a subsequent occasion. Thus, if it is scorching hot today, tomorrow will probably be cooler. Tall parents, on the average, have children shorter than they, and short parents on the average have children taller than they. People selected because they score low on an intelligence test will very likely score higher as a group on a subsequent administration of the test. If we introduce an intervention in a situation for which regression is plausible, we run the risk of ascribing the regression effects to the intervention—that is, in the last example, perceiving benefits in a program aimed at helping "dull" students to catch up when they have not really changed. (Regression, like instability, is a product of chance, but unlike instability, it has a predictable direction.) Regression is a plausible explanation of changes observed in a situation that is chosen for its extremity. Unfortunately, from the viewpoint of evaluation, policy interventions are frequently undertaken precisely when the level of a problem is abnormal or extreme.

The Classical Experiment

Scientifically acceptable evaluation of an intervention requires a methodology that renders explanations of changes by rival hypotheses implausible, thus supporting the theoretical explanation. This may be accomplished by ad hoc investigation of particular hypotheses in given cases—for example, by determining through special investigations whether new highways have been opened or favorable weather prevails in Ruritania. However, additional investigations are necessary to the extent that critics return with additional plausible alternative explanations. It is better to search for a study design that renders entire categories of rival hypotheses implausible—for instance, by subtracting their effect from the total change to be explained. The classical experiment is one such design.

In the classical experiment, an intervention is applied to individuals or subgroups at random. Those experiencing the intervention compose the experimental group. An equivalent control group is created by withholding the intervention from randomly chosen individuals or subgroups.

One could conceive of a classical experimental study of drinking-and-driving law in which, say, numerous counties would be assigned at random to either experimental or control groups and in which the relevant laws would be changed in the former areas but not in the latter. The classical experiment would compare changes in the experimental group with changes in the control group. History (that is, specific events other than legal differences) would be felt more or less equally in both sets of counties, as would maturation (that is, general trends). The random division of counties between experimental and control groups would assure that if regression were present, it would affect both groups. (I will not attempt to discuss here subtler problems such as possible interactions between history and the intervention.)

The use of numerous jurisdictions might also yield data concerning the magnitude of routine changes in the effect variable over the time period in question, thus enabling the researcher to estimate, through tests of statistical significance, whether instability is a plausible rival hypothesis under the circumstances. In short, if it were possible to introduce the new law as prescribed by the classical experimental model, it would be possible to come to a scientifically acceptable conclusion that the differences observed between the experimental and control groups were not explicable by the rival hypotheses considered and that the theoretical explanation was therefore supported.

The experimental model, for reasons of practicality and ethics, is rarely usable for studies of innovations in the formal law. It is, however, useful for studying variations in law enforcement. An example of such a study in general criminology is the Kansas City police-patrol experiment (Kelling and Pate 1974), which randomly assigned different levels of police patrol to different segments of the city to see whether the populations of the heavily patrolled areas reported less criminal victimization (they did not, but the study has been criticized for failing to vary the patrol conditions sufficiently).

Similar designs, although less elegantly controlled, appear in the traffic literature (OECD 1974; Fennessy et al. 1968). For instance, studies of the effect of patrol devices on speed often have included matched comparison road segments (Shumate 1961; California Highway Patrol 1966). An elegant experimental design recently was utilized to show the effect of enforcement of the 55-mph speed limit (Klein 1981). Studies of specific deterrence of violators also have manipulated actual sanction threats in an experimental manner (Blumenthal and Ross 1973; Ross and Blumenthal 1975). As seen in chapter 5, experimental design can be used to study effects of variations in the amount of police patrol in the drinking-and-driving area (Cameron, Strang, and Vulcan 1980), although the principle of randomness in patrol is a divisive political issue in many countries and truly random law enforcement is rare (Havard 1977).

Correlational Studies

The study of deterrence has not utilized experimental methodology to an important degree. Instead, the most common methodology is correlational (or econometric) analysis of natural variations in actual levels of punishments among different jurisdictions, usually American states. For example, observers might find that states with higher imprisonment rates (certainty of punishment) or longer prison sentences (severity of punishment) on the average have lower crime rates, controlling statistically for the influence of possible extraneous crime-related variables such as industrialization, unemployment, income, and proportion of minorities. On the basis of this finding, support for deterrence theory may be claimed. In fact, the results of this large literature have usually supported the deterrence model for traditional criminality, especially in the matters of certainty (the probability of arrest and/or conviction) and severity (Cook 1979, p. 29). A special case in this literature is the death penalty, which less-rigorous research has declared inferior in deterrent effectiveness to its alternatives but which some recent studies have endorsed.

However, the methodology of these studies has been strongly criticized, most recently by the prestigious panel of the National Academy of Sciences (Blumstein, Cohen, and Nagin 1978), which found nearly insuperable technical problems due to errors in measuring the crime rate, the confounding of incapacitation and deterrence, and the possibility that the level of crime affects sanctions in addition to sanctions' affecting crime. For these reasons the panel concluded, "We cannot yet assert that the evidence warrants an affirmative conclusion regarding deterrence" in general, and specifically "available studies provide no useful evidence on the deterrent effect of capital punishment" (pp. 7-9).

Despite the overwhelming predominance of correlational studies in the deterrence literature relating to general criminality, the correlational method has been very little used in the study of traffic law—a notable exception being the Votey studies (1978) of Scandinavian drinking-and-driving legislation—so the disrepute cast on the method by the academy's report has little import for the state of knowledge concerning deterrence of drivers.

Interrupted Time Series

A more-promising methodology is available in the form of quasi-experimental analyses of cases of deterrence-based interventions. However, many less-sophisticated case studies are flawed because they consist merely of descriptions of the intervention coupled with measures of the target behavior at a single point before, and at one point after, the intervention. To ascribe an observed change to the intervention under these circumstances is to ignore, among other things, the rival explanations provided by history, maturation, instability, and regression, described previously. However, this simple but faulty methodology often can be improved upon by adding more observation points for several time intervals prior and subsequent to the intervention. The resulting methodology is termed *interrupted time-series analysis*. It is useful in situations in which an intervention is expected to have a sharp, sudden impact and in which valid measurement of the effect variable extends for a considerable period of time on either side of the intervention. This is frequently the case for deterrence-based legal interventions.

Interrupted time-series analysis controls the situation for possible maturation effects by analyzing the entire data series for the presence of long-term trends. It controls for instability by utilizing the entire set of observations to calculate a significance level for the difference at the intervention point, using statistical tests specifically devised for the situation (McCleary and Hay 1980; McCain and McCleary 1979). It controls for regression by verifying the level of the series, whether normal or extreme, at the time of the intervention. Finally, although the interrupted time series does not by itself control for history, it can be supplemented with additional data (for example, from similar jurisdictions or during selected hours) to produce a model, termed *multiple time series*, that can adequately control for history.

The usefulness of interrupted time-series analysis in investigating a deterrence-based intervention and controlling for rival hypotheses is illustrated in the U.S. Department of Transportation's study (1980) of the adoption and repeal of mandatory motorcycle-rider helmet laws. Figure 3-1 is reproduced from this report. It documents changes in the crash-fatality rates for motorcycles during the adoption of helmet laws in forty-seven states between 1966 and 1975 and after subsequent repeal of such laws in

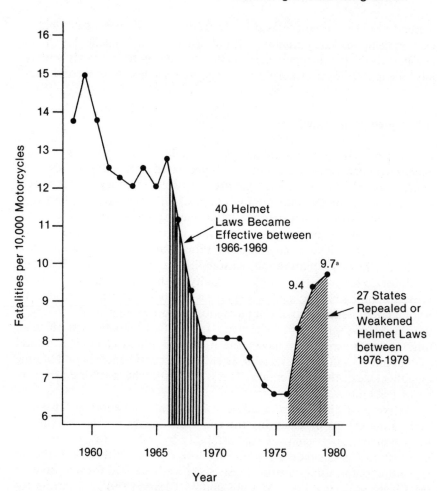

Source: U.S. Department of Transportation 1980, p. II-3.
aEstimated.

Figure 3-1. Motorcycle Fatalities per 10,000 Motorcycles

twenty-seven states. The 1966-1969 decline and the 1976-1979 rise in fatalities are clearly unusual events in the series, and neither can be explained easily in terms of preexisting trends (the earlier decline is exceptionally steep, and the later rise opposes the entire earlier trend). The initial intervention had its inception at a time when deaths were declining and not at an extremely high point. The juxtaposition of theoretically predicted responses to the two opposite interventions argues that this is not a product of unrelated historical events. Additional support for the theoretical explanation of these changes comes from a special observational study in four states that repealed the compulsory motorcycle-rider helmet laws, which found the proportion of cyclists wearing helmets to have declined from nearly 100 percent during the law's existence to about 50 percent after its repeal.

Conclusion

In sum, the study of deterrence-based interventions directed at drinking and driving permits analysts to use a set of relatively valid and inexpensive measures in the context of a methodological model that often can control for the effects of irrelevant factors that trouble research on more-traditional criminality. As such, this research has the capacity not only to enlighten policy with respect to the social problem of drinking and driving but also to add to understanding of the capabilities and limitations of law as an instrument of social control in general.

4 Scandinavian-Type Laws

For several decades, advocates of the deterrence approach to controlling drinking and driving have had in mind the model provided by the laws of Norway and Sweden. A widespread impression that the Scandinavians had developed a legal approach that, through its conformity to the deterrence model, had resolved or largely ameliorated the drinking-and-driving problem led to imitative laws in numerous countries. The impact of many adoptions of Scandinavian-type laws has been scientifically evaluated, and the accumulated reports furnish a basis for evaluating the deterrence model in general and the Scandinavian approach in particular.

This chapter surveys the evaluative literature. It begins with an exposition of the original Norwegian and Swedish laws. Subsequent adoptions of similar laws in the United Kingdom, on the European continent, in Australia and New Zealand, and in North America are traced, and the evaluation results are presented. The chapter then returns to the matter of evaluating the original Scandinavian laws in their home countries.

The Scandinavian Approach

In chapter 1, I noted that initial legal attempts to deal with the problem of drinking and driving everywhere followed a classical model. Classical laws proved to be unsatisfactory responses to the problem. Their traditional criminal-law-based concepts ignored a substantial share of the problem—namely, the drivers whose crash risk was importantly increased by alcohol but who showed no clinical signs of intoxication. Moreover, their criminal-law-based procedures made it difficult to apprehend and punish even those offenders who appeared to fall clearly within proscriptions. Drivers with subclinical blood-alcohol concentrations were not included in the population addressed by these laws, and even grossly intoxicated drivers (if they had caused no harm) could count on the vagueness of the legal concepts, and the prodefendant biases of Western criminal procedure, to lower their chances of accusation and conviction.

The legal history of nearly all countries shows continual and unsuccessful attempts to modify classical laws to produce increments of deterrence. A major difficulty in this endeavor was the very low actual probability of any punishment. In the language of the deterrence model, certainty of punishment was negligible, even for the grossly intoxicated driver. The fraction of impaired trips leading to an encounter with a policeman was miniscule, and the fraction of these in turn leading to prosecution and conviction was very small.

Classical laws were often defective from the deterrence viewpoint because of low severity of punishment as well as low certainty. For instance, even in Sweden the punishment for drinking and driving originally, and for many years, was limited to licensing actions that, in the context of a poor society without many automobiles, could be regarded as relatively mild. Legislatures and courts in most countries were loath to apply imprisonment for traffic offenses, including drinking and driving, when no immediate harm had been done.

Furthermore, classical laws were slow in delivering punishment. Until the development of modern court management and streamlining of the processing of voluminous charges related to traffic, drivers could expect considerable lags in their interaction with the legal system, which compromised the principle of celerity of punishment.

A new approach to drinking-and-driving law was introduced in Norway and Sweden just before World War II. Although its formulation was aided by Scandinavian scientists who were developing the technology for measuring blood-alcohol concentrations, the new approach was implemented in large part because of a politically powerful and moralistic temperance movement that was willing to blame almost any social ill on alcohol. As noted by Andenaes:

> In the Storting [Norwegian Parliament] rather strong expressions were used about the role played by alcohol. In 1930 the Storting's Road Committee stated that "a deplorably large part of the accidents that occur through driving an automobile are caused by the driver being under the influence of alcohol." During the legislative proceedings in 1935 several speakers dwelt upon the same theme. One member said, "One can examine the police reports and see how large a part of the accidents that have occurred on the roads in connection with the driving of a motor vehicle have happened because of drunkenness. . . ." Another said, "I know that the most serious traffic accidents in this country occur because of alcohol. At least 75 percent of the accidents occur because the drivers have been drunk." . . . It seems that none of the speakers had any systematic material on which to base their statements. And these statements contrast strangely with the information given in the annual reports of the Oslo police. . . . The statements rather show what a loose foundation the legislators were building on. [1978, p. 47-48]

On this loose foundation, the Norwegian Parliament constructed a drinking-and-driving law that, with minor modifications, remains in force to this day. Compared to classical law, the Norwegian legislation of 1936 appears better to conform to the principles of deterrence. The most radical change in the law was to define the culpable act as driving with a blood-alcohol concentration in excess of 50 milligrams per 100 milliliters of blood (0.05 percent in U.S. notation). This provision is often referred to as a per se rule. The need to define and prove that a driver was drunk or under the influence of alcohol was obviated, and the new criterion was clothed in the mantle of science.

A likely result of this definition was an increase in certainty of punishment for drinking drivers, resulting primarily from simplification of conviction for those charged. By itself, the redefinition of the offense of drinking and driving might not have been expected to affect apprehension. However, the practice by Norwegian police of verifying drivers' licenses and insurance papers in "random" roadblocks, coupled with the availability of breath-testing devices in the event of the odor of alcoholic beverages, very likely made it easier to apprehend the drinking driver under the new law.

Sweden introduced fixed blood-alcohol criteria for drinking and driving in 1941, a few years after Norway. The Swedish law differed primarily in that it established two levels of violation: one for blood-alcohol concentrations between 80 and 149 milligrams/100 milliliters, and a second at 150 milligrams and over; each of these levels carried a different degree of punishment.

Although the Swedish prohibition covered a smaller sector of the alcohol-involvement scale than its Norwegian counterpart, it was designed to produce the same effect on the more-limited population being addressed. With the exception of lowering the lesser-offense limit to 50 milligrams, the Swedish law, like the Norwegian, remains basically the same today. However, the impression of certainty of apprehension in Sweden may have been affected positively by rules passed provisionally in 1974 and permanently in 1976, permitting police to demand screening breath tests for blood alcohol without restrictions in the course of scheduled roadblocks, as well as in connection with crashes and certain traffic violations.

The redefinition of the drinking-and-driving offense was accomplished in both Sweden and Norway on the basis of prior statutes prescribing relatively severe punishments for the offense. Thus, the Scandinavian approach is characterized by severity as well as relative certainty of punishment. In Sweden, the penalty, in the absence of very rare extenuating circumstances, is one month's imprisonment for the more-serious offense and heavy fines for the less-serious one. License revocation applies to both offenses. Imprisonment and license suspension routinely apply to the single-level Norwegian offense in a similar manner.

No information is reported concerning the celerity with which punishment of drinking drivers is achieved in Norway and Sweden. However, prompt administrative action to suspend the driver's license is very much a part of the approach.

In short, the Norwegian legislation of 1936 and the Swedish legislation of 1941 furnish a model for controlling drinking drivers. The model has served as the basis for replacing classical laws in many countries. Fundamental to this model is a redefinition of the offense and subsequent mode of proof—that is, the model refers to blood-alcohol concentrations rather than subjective descriptions of intoxicated behavior. The model also provides sanctions considered severe and depriving, such as imprisonment and loss of license, and promptness in the disposition of at least some aspects of pending cases. These characteristics of the law are in accord with practical suggestions for behavior control derived from the theoretical model of deterrence.

I shall reserve until a later section a discussion of the evidence concerning the deterrent effectiveness of the Norwegian and Swedish laws. It may suffice here to indicate that the large majority of alcohol and traffic experts and government officials in Scandinavia have made strong claims for the effectiveness of their laws, at least in part because of the laws' conformity to the deterrence model. Such cautions and complexities as may have been offered with these claims usually have been lost in the process of international communication, and adoptions of Scandinavian-type laws in other countries after World War II usually have been promoted by arguments that assumed the impressive success of Swedish and Norwegian laws in their home countries.

Reliable evaluations of the effectiveness of the Scandinavian approach to drinking-and-driving law may be better accomplished by studying more-recent adoptions of this type of law in countries other than Norway and Sweden.

United Kingdom

In the Road Safety Act of 1967, the British Parliament adopted Scandinavian-type legislation, affecting drinking drivers. This represented one of the first important adoptions of the model outside the northern countries, and it furnished the first large-scale example of the effectiveness of such legislation in deterring drinking and driving. The apparent success of the British law stimulated the subsequent adoption of similar laws in nations all over the world.

Unlike the Scandinavian originals and some subsequent laws, the British legislation had its inception at a fortunate time for analysis. The drinking-and-driving problem in the United Kingdom was at a chronic rather than an acute level, eliminating the issue of regression or return to normality as a plausible explanation for any decline in subsequent crashes. U.K. statistical series concerning crashes, fatalities, and related matters were of good quality and were available in considerable detail for several years before and after the inception of the legislation. No other important laws promising reductions in crashes were adopted at or near the same time. Particularly fortunate is the fact that the 1967 law preceded by several years the strong disruption in world traffic patterns occasioned by the 1973 fuel crisis, which has interfered with evaluations of many subsequent traffic-safety innovations. Finally, sufficient time has now passed so that further experience will have little effect on conclusions concerning the law's aftermath. The book is now closed on the British Road Safety Act of 1967.

There have been several analyses of this law performed under the aegis of the governmentally sponsored Transport and Road Research Laboratory (see, for example, Sabey and Codling 1975; Saunders 1975). However, in the following pages I shall rely principally on the evaluation that I carried out, with the technical assistance of Leslie McCain, on data gathered during a visit to England in 1971 (Ross 1973).

Prior to 1967, the approach to drinking and driving in the United Kingdom had taken the form of modified classical legislation. Its chief foundations were the Road Traffic Acts of 1960 and 1962. The former defined the violation as being "unfit to drive through drink or drugs," and the latter violation was driving when the "ability to drive properly is for the time being impaired." The 1962 law had been adopted under the goading of the British Medical Association, which viewed drinking and driving as a health problem and which was impatient with the inefficacy of existing legal controls. In particular, the association was appalled by the difficulty in obtaining convictions of drivers charged before juries (Ross 1973, p. 13). Problems of identifying and appraising drinking drivers by police and magistrates were also noted.

Compared to its predecessor, the 1962 act took steps toward increasing both the certainty and severity of legal threats against drinking drivers. With respect to severity, an important contribution was to specify a year's mandatory license suspension for serious motoring offenses, a category in which drinking and driving was included. With respect to certainty of punishment, the act introduced the use of chemical tests for blood-alcohol concentrations and required that courts should:

[H]ave regard to any evidence which may be given of the proportion or quantity of alcohol or of any drug which was contained in the blood or present in the body of the accused, as ascertained by analysis . . . of a specimen of blood taken from him with his consent by a medical practitioner, or of urine . . . ; and if it is proved that the accused when so requested by a constable at any time, refused to consent to the taking of or to provide a specimen for analysis . . . his refusal may, unless reasonable cause therefore is shown, be treated as supporting any evidence given on behalf of the prosecution, or as rebutting any evidence given on behalf of the defense, with respect to his condition at the time. [Ross 1973, p. 14]

Experience following the act of 1962 did not lead to a conclusion of deterrent effectiveness. The blood-test data merely proved what had been suspected before—that drivers with very high blood-alcohol concentrations stood a good chance of escaping conviction because of jury sympathy and the inherent vagueness of the classical definition of the offense of drinking and driving. The 1962 law did not provide a fixed level of blood alcohol for conviction, and no legally compelling way existed of relat'ng blood-test data to the criterion of impairment. These data usually were translated before the court into estimates of actual consumption of beverages according to a highly conservative table of equivalents. Furthermore, the 1962 legislation placed no penalty on a driver for refusing to provide a blood or urine specimen other than that the fact could be noted in court.

The British Medical Association was discouraged by the demonstrated inability of the 1962 law to convict drivers with high blood-alcohol concentrations and was prodded to further efforts by the availability of new research concerning the increased crash risk of drinking drivers (Ross 1973, p. 15). As a result, the association put its full weight behind a proposal, consciously modeled on the Scandinavian approach, embodying fixed blood-alcohol limits, compulsory blood tests, and random stops by police for screening purposes. It persuaded the minister of transport, Mrs. Barbara Castle, to work for enactment of this legislation.

The principle of "random," or arbitrary, police stops to test drivers for blood alcohol, although clearly compatible with deterrence principles, was at the time unprecedented—even in Scandinavia—and was so strongly resisted in the United Kingdom on civil-libertarian grounds that the government withdrew this provision from the proposed law. Instead, permission to demand a screening test was made contingent on the accused's being involved in an accident, having a moving-traffic violation, or giving reasonable cause for a police officer to suspect alcohol in the body. As noted by Mrs. Castle in Parliament, the retreat from random testing was not complete:

> What we have done is to concentrate the operation of the random principle so that those who can now be required to take a roadside test are more likely to include offenders. . . . It will be apparent to hon. Members that these tests will still be random in a very important sense. Accidents can happen to all of us. [Ross 1973, p. 19]

Despite points of disagreement about the proposed law—including impairment of relations between police and the public, undesirable denial of discretion to judges, undue severity of punishment (license suspension) for borderline cases or for those whose living depended on driving, possible harassment of ordinary social drinkers at pubs, and possible errors in testing—no important changes other than those involving provisions for random testing were made in the bill. It received Royal Assent on 11 May 1967 and became effective on 9 October 1967 (the act applied only to England and Wales, and subsequent data and discussion refer to these jurisdictions).

The Road Safety Act of 1967 brought two major changes to existing British legislation on drinking and driving. First, it created the offenses of driving or attempting to drive and being in charge of a motor vehicle on a road or other public place, "having consumed alcohol in such a quantity that the proportion thereof in his blood, as ascertained by a laboratory test for which he subsequently provides a specimen . . . exceeds the prescribed limit," which was set at 80 milligrams/100 milliliters (0.08 percent in U.S. notation). Second, it permitted police to demand a screening breath test under the aforementioned conditions. Failure of the breath test or unreasonable refusal subjected the accused to the requirement of a second screening breath test at a police station and eventually to a blood test for evidence admissible in court. Refusal to take part in the tests was punishable as though the tests had been failed.

It is worthwhile to note that the Road Safety Act of 1967 did not increase the severity of the penalty for drinking and driving. The most feared punishment was a year's license suspension (disqualification), which had been enacted in 1962. In practice, the courts added little in the way of additional punishment, other than nominal fines, for violation of the 1967 act.

That the Road Safety Act was controversial before and after its adoption is, in my opinion, a crucial fact. The widespread initial hostility to the proposed legislation, based largely on provisions for random testing, has already been mentioned. Although this hostility sufficed to modify the random test, it was not enough to deflect the government from enacting the remaining provisions.

Opposition continued strong for months and years. Antipathy to the legislation was common even among police and judges. Police applied the law in a sparing and restrained way that surprised the government, which had to throw out hundreds of thousands of screening breath-test devices that had passed their expiration dates without use. Following the ruling in *Scott* v. *Baker* [2 All E.R. 993 (Q.B. 1968)] that the validity of the blood test in court depended on the prosecution's strict adherence to the required procedure in every detail, judges produced a wealth of decisions favoring defendants on the basis of technicalities. The ruling allowed defense counsel to search through a complicated procedure for substantively unimportant but technically valid objections to police activity, creating a crisis in police morale and suggesting to the government that further legislation would be needed (Ross 1973, pp. 50-62). In one case, the divisional court ruled that a person arriving home while hotly pursued by the police had ceased to be a driver within the meaning of the act and could not legitimately be asked for a breath test. Likewise, a person stopping temporarily—to make a telephone call, to visit the toilet, to talk with a passenger, and so on—was held to be not driving. The provision that the screening breath test be made "there or nearby" also was narrowly interpreted; when the arresting policeman was without a test kit, a voluntary walk by the accused of 160 yards toward a police station was held to violate this provision of the law.

The legal interpretation in these cases was liberalized, and the legislation saved, by subsequent decisions in the court of appeal and the House of Lords. However, several loopholes remained, including the famous hip-flask defense in which the suspect consumed additional liquor to calm his nerves after being involved in an accident and before the arrival of the police.

From the viewpoint of the government, these difficulties were sad testimonials to the intransigence and stubbornness of officialdom, sabotaging virtuous legislation aimed at saving lives. From the viewpoint of the deterrence mechanism, however, these difficulties were an unforeseen and essential boon. The Road Safety Act was news (the provisions of the Road Safety Act of 1967, now incorporated into the Road Traffic Act of 1972, have continued to generate controversy about the balance between individual liberty and the public interest). At the inception of the act, the government had spent £350,000 on a publicity campaign, including preparing and circulating a leaflet on the law and publicizing its provisions on television and in other media. However, this campaign was limited in duration, and although surveys at the time showed that people were made aware of the law, it is not clear that official publicity alone could have created and maintained the impression of certain and severe punishment.

In my opinion, it is very likely that sustained attention to the law, in large part because of the difficulties mentioned earlier, helped to achieve and maintain a perception of increased threat. This is particularly likely in view of the relatively modest activity of the U.K. police. The number of tests per month went from about 3,000 in 1967 to about 7,000-8,000 by early 1971. During all of 1970, approximately 70,000 breath tests were given in the United Kingdom. This contrasts with 48,000 in Sweden in the same year—even though the population of Sweden was less than one-sixth that of England and Wales—and 93,000 in Los Angeles County, with a population of 7 million compared to 58 million in the United Kingdom. It is likely that the threat posed by the Road Safety Act was considerably magnified for an extended period of time by the newsworthiness of its loopholes and failures.

Road casualties declined impressively in the months after the inception of the British legislation. Officialdom, in a properly restrained manner, implied that the drop may well have been due to the law. More-involved parties, such as the temperance movement, were less restrained in their claims. One writer was willing to conclude that the experience of five days surrounding Christmas 1967, compared with the previous year, "provided sufficient proof" that the law was justified (Ross 1973, p. 21). Such claims are scientifically irresponsible because they ignore possible differences in weather and similar factors, the possibility of random variation, and other methodological problems noted earlier in this book.

However, application of an adequate methodology—specifically, interrupted time-series analysis—to a longer series of data from the United Kingdom does strongly support the claim that the Road Safety Act of 1967 had a deterrent effect on drinking and driving. Some of this evidence is diagramed in figures 4-1 and 4-2, which present crash casualty and fatality rates, adjusted for mileage, during the period 1961-1970. (These data have been corrected for the number of days in the month, and a marked seasonal variation has been removed by an averaging process; see Ross 1973, p. 30.) Although the scale of these figures does not highlight the change in October 1967, the drop is visible, and statistical tests show it to be significant—that is, the change in the level of the curve was not merely random. The fact that the drop is greater in figure 4-2 than in figure 4-1 supports the interpretation that the drop was due to the drinking-and-driving law because we know that alcohol is more involved in fatal crashes than in crashes in general.

Further evidence that the change was due to the law rather than to some simultaneous historical event is presented by the data in figure 4-3, concerning fatal and serious-injury crashes on weekend nights. (Corrections for weekends per month and seasonality have been made in these figures, but

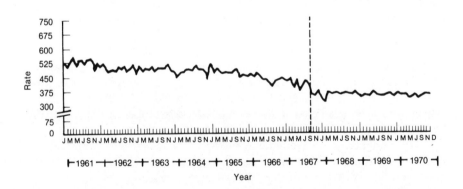

Figure 4-1. Total Casualties per 100-Million Vehicle Miles in the United Kingdom, Corrected for Month and with Seasonal Variations Removed

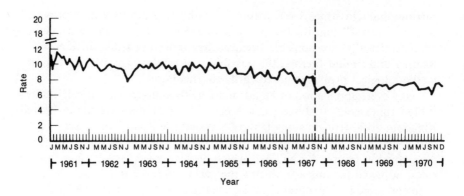

Figure 4-2. U.K. Fatality Rate, Corrected for Month and with Seasonal Variations Removed

because mileage figures specific to the hour of day are not available, these graphs are presented in terms of incidents rather than rates.) Alcohol is much more commonly involved in weekend-night crashes than in crashes at other times, rendering series like this particularly sensitive indicators of drinking and driving. The effect of the Road Safety Act is clearly visible here. The September-October drop is 66 percent, an unprecedented and highly significant decline.

The series in figure 4-3 may be compared with that in figure 4-4, which presents similar data for weekday commuting hours when alcohol is relatively rarely involved in crashes. The curve in figure 4-4 shows a small and nonsignificant drop, easily attributable to chance. The comparison of the curves strongly supports the interpretation that the reduction in total casualties is largely explained by a reduction in alcohol-related casualties, which would be predicted if the Road Safety Act operated through the mechanism of simple deterrence.

Additional data are available to support this deterrence interpretation. Change was found neither in the number of miles traveled coincident with the Road Safety Act nor in the sales of alcoholic beverages. However, a comparison of results from surveys of drivers in September 1967, before the law took effect, and in January 1968, after it had been in effect for three months, reveals that there was a decline from 60 to 48 percent in the number of drivers admitting to combining drinking and driving. There also was an increase in the number of people reportedly walking to their drinking places; this increase was largest for drinkers in pubs. Prior to the 1967 law, 49 percent reported returning from the pub by car, whereas after the law the percentage was 37 (Ross 1973, p. 65).

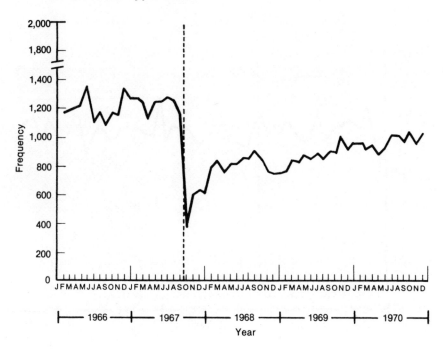

Figure 4-3. Fatalities and Serious Injuries in the United Kingdom, Combined for Friday Nights, 10 P.M. to Midnight; Saturday Mornings, Midnight to 4 A.M.; Saturday Nights, 10 P.M. to Midnight; and Sunday Mornings, Midnight to 4 A.M.; Corrected for Weekend Days per Month and with Seasonal Variations Removed

Other evidence comes from blood-alcohol statistics based on tests made of samples of all drivers killed in crashes in England and Wales. The sampling was fairly complete (Ross 1979). From December 1966 to September 1967 (prior to the inception of the legislation), 25 percent of the drivers killed had illegal blood-alcohol concentrations. This declined to 15 percent in the corresponding period of 1967-1968. These independent data lend support to the interpretation that the Road Safety Act of 1967, through its effect on perceived threat of punishment, caused people to separate drinking and driving, resulting in the saving of many lives (Ross 1973, p. 66).

Although evidence is strong that the Road Safety Act was initially effective, it is now equally clear that this effect dissipated within a few years. Evidence of this dissipation appears in figures 4-1 and 4-2, which show the

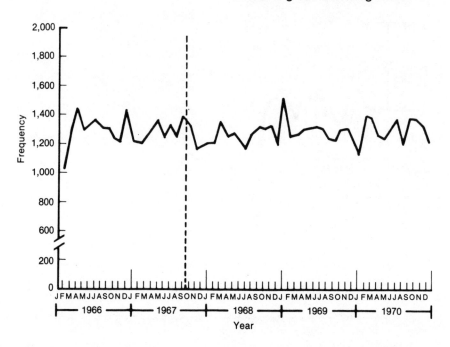

Source: Ross 1973, p. 34. Copyright by The University of Chicago Press. Reprinted with permission.

Figure 4-4. Fatalities and Serious Injuries in the United Kingdom, Combined for Mondays through Fridays, 7 A.M. to 10 A.M. and 4 P.M. to 5 P.M., Corrected for Weekdays per Month and with Seasonal Variations Removed

initial effectiveness of the 1967 law in the simultaneous drops in crashes and fatalities. The curves show not only a change in level in October 1967 but also a change in slope. The curve of total casualties fell less steeply after 1967, and the curve of fatalities actually changed direction from a decline to an increase. Both of these changes are statistically significant (Ross 1973, pp. 30-32). Extrapolation of either curve predicts that, without further change, the initial casualty savings would disappear over time. The same prediction can be made from the curve in figure 4-3, which is based on more-specialized data.

No further research has been reported using precisely the data underlying these curves. However, U.K. sources have confirmed the conclusion of diminished effect using related data series such as the proportion of casualties during the main drinking hours of 10 P.M. to 4 A.M. (on all nights) and the blood-alcohol concentrations in drivers killed in crashes.

Table 4-1 reports the former percentages through mid-1973 (Sabey and Codling 1975, p. 75). Table 4-2 reports the percentages of drivers with illegal blood-alcohol concentrations through 1976 (Sabey 1978, p. 192). On the basis of these data, U.K. experts have concluded that, "in short, the effect of the act is wearing off" (Saunders 1975, p. 845).

One can look, as did Saunders, for the origin of this loss of effectiveness in social trends such as increasing alcohol consumption due to changes in the real price of alcoholic beverages and changes in the size and distribution of national income. However, inspection of data from the early years of the act indicates that deterrence was being accomplished without a decline in alcohol consumption, apparently because drinking was being separated from driving. There is no reason why the same phenomenon could not take place even with an increase in alcohol consumption.

There is a more-plausible explanation for the long-run failure of the Road Safety Act. The deterrence model suggests that U.K. drivers separated their drinking and driving following passage of the legislation because they feared that there was now a realistic likelihood of being punished. There is no empirical evidence concerning the development of this belief, but it is reasonable to infer in light of the historical events detailed previously. Yet the real chances that a drinking driver would be caught, charged, and convicted in the United Kingdom, although much increased, never reached a very high absolute level. The gap was not in the matter of conviction—the vast majority of those charged with drinking and driving was convicted (Saunders 1975, p. 851)—but rather in the probability of being charged. I calculated that in 1970 the probability of undergoing a breath test in the United Kingdom was about one for every two million vehicle miles driven. Although the number of breath tests administered since that time has increased, the chances of being tested still are on the order of one in a million miles (since the tests are selectively administered, the chances of a drunk driver being tested are probably higher). Although there is insufficient evidence to evaluate the certainty of the legal threat with precision, it appears to be very low by any reasonable criterion.

The initial publicity campaigns and newsworthiness surrounding the Road Safety Act made the legislation very well known. They also very likely

Table 4-1
Percentages of U.K. Casualties in the Main Drinking Hours (10 P.M.-4 A.M.)

	1966-1967	1967-1968	1968-1969	1969-1970	1970-1971	1971-1972	1972-1973
Killed	28.3	21.3	22.5	24.3	25.0	25.7	26.2
Injured	21.2	15.6	17.1	18.1	19.0	19.1	19.8

Source: Sabey and Codling 1975, p. 75.

Table 4-2
Percentage of Fatally Injured Drivers in the United Kingdom with Blood-Alcohol Concentrations Exceeding 80 milligrams/100 milliliters

1967 (to September)	1968	1969	1970	1971	1972	1973	1974	1975	1976
32	20	25	23	27	30	33	36	38	38

Source: Sabey 1978, p. 192.

gave a grossly exaggerated picture of the certainty of apprehension that might be expected by a drinking driver in England and Wales. I believe that this exaggerated perception of certainty, coupled with severe punishment, resulted in the impressive, albeit short-term, deterrent effectiveness of the act. It seems reasonable to me to ascribe the subsequently rising curves of casualties and of alcohol-related deaths to the gradual learning by U.K. drivers that they had overestimated the certainty of punishment under the new law. The obvious benefits of drinking and driving—inexpensive and convenient transportation in connection with a normal, alcohol-related social life—overwhelmed the deterrent efficacy of the British Road Safety Act.

France

The French law of 12 July 1978 is among the most recent adoptions of the Scandinavian approach to drinking-and-driving law. Both the nature of the law and its context make it an interesting case study. It was the first adoption of the Scandinavian approach abroad to provide for the breath testing of all drivers passing through roadblocks scheduled for this purpose (the "random" testing originally proposed in the United Kingdom). The French law thus is capable of demonstrating what might occur with a technique that promises important increments of certainty of apprehension for drinking drivers. Furthermore, the centrality of alcohol consumption to French culture makes France a particularly interesting test case for the capabilities of a law restricting drinking, at least in certain contexts. The threat of roadblock testing suggests the possibility of an important effect, whereas the conflict with cultural prescriptions dampens these expectations.

Unlike the U.K. case, no overall scientific evaluations of the French experience have been made by official observers. The discussion that follows is based principally on data obtained during visits I made to France in the summer of 1979 and the fall of 1980. The analysis was performed with the technical assistance of Richard McCleary and Thomas Epperlein (Ross, McCleary, and Epperlein 1982).

The 1978 French law was in some ways a less-extreme innovation than the British Road Safety Act, since many aspects of the Scandinavian approach to drinking and driving had been adopted in France over the years. The testing of breath for alcohol was made possible in France in 1965, in the case of major violations of traffic law, and was made compulsory in the case of certain violations and crashes in 1970. The 1970 law also created the offense of driving with a blood-alcohol concentration in excess of 0.8 grams pro mille (0.08 percent), the punishment for which could include suspension of the driver's license. However, a crash-related death toll of 15,000 per year in France did not permit complacency, and various projects to strengthen the deterrent effect of the law were proposed in Parliament during the next decade.

Whereas in the United Kingdom the medical association led the initiative to obtain Scandinavian-type legislation, in France it was the Interministerial Committee for Road Safety, a governmental organization founded in 1972, comparable in functions to the U.S. National Highway Traffic Safety Administration and headed by an ambitious and energetic civil servant, Christian Gérondeau. After apparently successful initiatives in reducing crash-related casualties through laws requiring seat-belt usage and through the imposition of speed limits, Gérondeau selected drinking and driving as the object of his next reform, with strong backing from the ministers of health and justice. He proposed to reinforce the 1970 law by requiring breath tests to determine blood-alcohol concentrations in drivers passing through roadblocks and by providing stiff penalties for violators, including mandatory license suspension under some circumstances.

Passage of this law in Parliament did not come smoothly, as might be expected given the interests at stake in both alcohol and automobiles in France. As in the United Kingdom, parliamentary debates focused on the proper balance between personal liberty and the public interest. The tests, the roadblocks, and the sanctions all were questioned, and the struggle was prolonged because major differences developed between the two Houses of Parliament, the Senate being more troubled by the civil-liberties implications of the legislation. However, the matter was ultimately resolved without need for significant compromise, and the Parliamentary struggle kept the pending legislation in the news.

The four main innovations of the law of 12 July 1978 were the following:

1. Any driver could be required to submit to a screening test for blood alcohol in the context of roadblock operations. These operations were to be ordered by the region's chief judicial officer and conducted by the police.
2. Failure of the screening test could result in an order to cease driving then and there, as well as imposition of penalties previously provided for the offense of driving with elevated blood alcohol.

3. A driver's license could be revoked—not merely suspended—as a consequence of being found guilty of driving with more than 0.8 pro mille blood-alcohol concentration; revocation was mandatory under certain circumstances.
4. Provision was made for replacement of the testing devices currently used with technologically superior ones when such devices would be approved by the authorities.

Thus, the legislation importantly reinforced existing law in matters of concern to deterrence theory. Based on either existing or novel provisions of French law, a screening breath test was obligatory for a driver or other person implicated in causing any injury-producing crash, for a driver accused of any of a large number of traffic-law violations, and for all drivers passing through scheduled roadblocks. Tests also were permitted in other circumstances at the discretion of the police. Moreover, the probability of a severe sanction—loss of license—was increased by the mandatory provisions of the new law, and the certainty and celerity of punishment were to be addressed, in time, by the use of better technology for testing blood-alcohol concentrations.

In France in 1978, as in the United Kingdom a decade earlier, officials immediately interpreted lower crash figures as evidence of the effectiveness of their legislation. The Interministerial Committee's newsletter in August headlined: "First effects of the law on alcohol—large drop in highway accidents in the month of July—175 fewer killed than in July 1977"; in September, "The decline is confirmed"; in October, "Towards a record year for highway safety—thanks to the Alcotest law, an exceptional summer."

However, again as in the United Kingdom, considerable vocal opposition came from beverage-industry groups, civil libertarians, and some driver groups. One beverage-industry organization characterized the new law as a declaration of war on the traditional beverage of the French people. The president of another held the official publicity campaign to be creating "a veritable psychosis of fear. . . . [I]ncredible terms have been uttered, the word Wine being sometimes associated with 'vice' or a plague." The libertarian reaction to the law can be characterized by the following open letter in a provincial newspaper from the director of the local university:

It is unthinkable that a State that calls itself liberal can treat Frenchmen as potential criminals, forced to justify themselves before witnesses. It is unthinkable that rulers originating from the people can submit the latter to suspicion joined with the violation of personal integrity which gives the operations their humiliating character. The faults of some people cannot justify the end of liberty for everyone. If this be not the case then, little by little, our entire lives will become the subject of police operations. [Ouest-France, September 20, 1978]

Although the large automobile clubs in France, unlike those in the United Kingdom, did not take a stand on the new law, opposition was led by the *Auto-Défense* movement, the creation of a traveling salesman from the provinces whose previous battles had included attacks on speed limits and seatbelt regulations. In a handbill, the president of this movement announced:

> . . . [C]reation of a National Committee to Fight the Alcotest. . . . It has brought a threat to the physical integrity of the individual taken at random and having committed no crime. . . . Adopted legally by Parliament but extorted from Parliamentarians by means of tendentious propaganda and falsified statistics, this law refuses to attack the real problem of alcoholism and has no other ends than to place the state's responsibility in highway matters upon the users of the highways.

The law's opponents, who prior to its passage had based their opposition on the lack of evidence in official statistics concerning the role of alcohol in crashes, continued their opposition based on findings that roadblock operations produced few positive breath tests. *Auto-Défense,* suing Gérondeau personally for diffusion of falsehoods, disputed his claims for effectiveness of the law on grounds that the decline in deaths was arbitrarily attributed to the law rather than to improvements in the highway network. Moreover, it was discovered that the testing devices used by the police were calibrated at the level of 0.5 pro mille, whereas the law permitted driving with blood-alcohol concentrations of up to 0.8 pro mille, and this fact had not been made known to the police or the public. However, the government maintained its position and made no compromises in the administration of the new law.

The persistence and reasonableness of the opposition's arguments, the implacability of the government in resisting these arguments, and official and unofficial publicity seem to have produced widespread public knowledge of the new drinking-and-driving law. The French Institute of Public Opinion found that 97 percent of a random sample of adults in August 1978 knew of the law, a record for familiarity with new legislation. In October, 66 percent could state the legal limit in response to a survey question. The law was popular in the abstract; its provisions were favored by nearly four to one in a poll in January 1979.

For the methodological reasons discussed, I agree with critics that the government was impetuous and premature in its initial claims of effectiveness for the law. However, during visits to France, I obtained a variety of data for interrupted time-series analysis of the French experience. On the basis of this analysis, it appears that deterrence was achieved, at least during the early months of the law's existence (Ross, McCleary, and Epperlein 1982). The analytical techniques permit estimation of the magnitude and duration of the deterrent effects in the series studied.

An example of this analysis appears in figure 4-5, a curve depicting crash-related injuries in France with seasonal variations statistically removed. The series of available data runs from 1973 to 1980. It shows a slight downward trend throughout the series. A sharp drop simultaneous with the new law is visually evident and is found to be statistically significant by appropriate tests. The drop in the series was initially approximately 12.5 percent of the average, but it is also visually evident that the drop was temporary and that the series returned to its previous trend. The deterrent effect was 95 percent dissipated in 8.4 months; in other words, the series had returned to within 5 percent of its preintervention normal course in less than nine months. While deterrence by the French law thus seems to have been temporary, it very likely prevented more than 11,000 injuries during its period of effectiveness.

Another illustration of this analysis appears in figure 4-6, depicting crash-related deaths in the same manner and for the same period as figure 4-5 for injuries. The drop at the inception of the law of 12 July 1978 is again

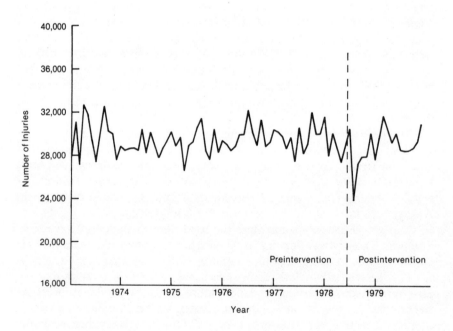

Source: Ross, McCleary, and Epperlein (1982).

Figure 4-5. Crash-Related Injuries in France with Seasonal Variations Removed

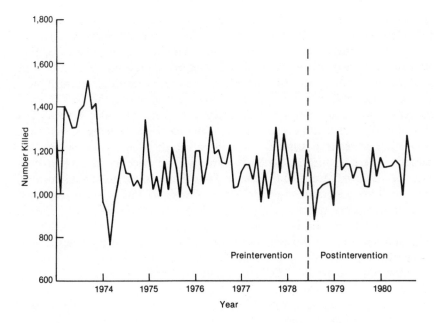

Source: Ross, McCleary, and Epperlein (1982).
Figure 4-6. Crash-Related Deaths in France with Seasonal Variations
              Removed

significant, and calculations show its initial magnitude as 13.9 percent.
Dissipation of the law's effectiveness took 12.9 months; nearly 700 lives
were saved due to the deterrent effect during these months. The percentage
drop in fatalities was greater and the dissipation period longer for fatalities
than for injuries, conforming to expectations based on the greater influence
of alcohol in fatal crashes than in injury-producing ones.

   Weekend-night crashes were also analyzed and compared with weekday
crashes, although on the basis of only partial and truncated data series that
could not be deseasonalized. Statistically significant declines of more than a
third were found in both injuries and deaths on weekends, compared to no
significant change for the weekday series. Likewise, there was a statistically
significant drop in crashes producing injury in two jurisdictions in northern
France noted for their high alcohol consumption, in contrast to no significant change in five jurisdictions in southern France noted for their low
alcohol consumption.

   It may be concluded that in France in 1978, as in the United Kingdom in
1967, a Scandinavian-type drinking-and-driving law reduced automobile

crashes and consequently injuries and deaths. As in the U.K. analysis, available data were searched for evidence of how this effect was accomplished —whether through reduced drinking, reduced driving, or both. The first possibility, reduced drinking, was addressed by submitting wholesale wine sales to interrupted time-series analysis, with negative results. Although these are not ideal indicators for total alcohol consumption, the lack of any noticeable decline in sales, along with related evidence provided in interviews with manufacturers and distributors of other alcoholic beverages, suggested that claims of reduced drinking—and threats to the viability of the beverage industry—were erroneous. Similarly, there was no evidence of decline in an index of kilometers traveled in France. Thus, I am led to the conclusion that, as in the United Kingdom, the combination of drinking and driving was reduced without noticeably affecting either drinking or driving separately.

My conclusions, based on the interrupted time-series analysis of French data, are supported by independent evidence from two French studies, one of which also confirms the impression that the effectiveness of the law disappeared within a year or so. The French National Organization for Road Safety (ONSER) utilized roadside-survey methods to study blood-alcohol concentrations among non-crash-involved drivers in 1977. The same organization mounted a comparable study in the spring of 1979, the year subsequent to the new law (DeBuhan and Filou 1979). Comparison of the results of the studies found that the proportion of drivers with illegal blood-alcohol concentrations dropped from 3.4 percent in the former to 1.8 percent in the latter. The detailed comparison finds some unexplained paradoxes—for example, the fact that illegal blood-alcohol concentrations were unaffected during the nighttime hours and even on weekend nights—but the general finding is impressive in magnitude and lends support to the conclusion of deterrence.

Also relevant are monthly figures compiled by Dr. Claude Got of Garches Hospital in suburban Paris, concerning blood-alcohol concentrations among all French drivers found responsible for fatal crashes. A special analysis was performed by Dr. Got at my request. Appropriate data were available only for those drivers who were blood tested but not breath tested (approximately one-quarter of the entire sample), and inferences must consequently be guarded. However, as indicated by the line in figure 4-7, the results are as expected according to the earlier interpretation. An abrupt decline occurred in the proportion of illegal blood-alcohol concentrations in this sample precisely coinciding with the new law. Within a few months, matters returned to their previous level.

The Got and ONSER studies are inconsistent in that the effect found by Got did not last to the end of 1978, whereas the postlaw ONSER study occurred several months into the following year. I am surprised by the shortness of the effect found by Got and by the length and depth of that reported by ONSER.

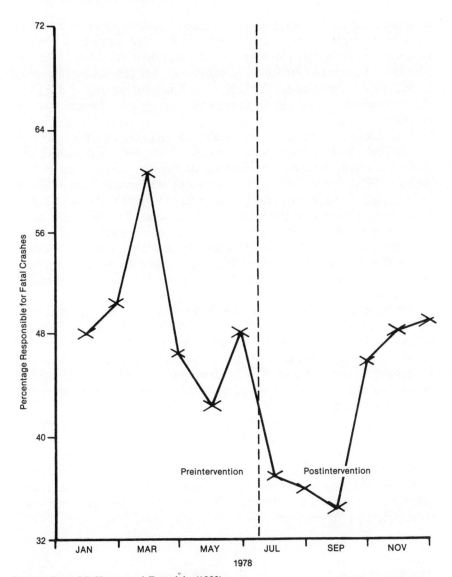

Source: Ross, McCleary, and Epperlein (1982).
Figure 4-7. Persons Responsible for Fatal Crashes in France with Illegal
Blood-Alcohol Concentrations

Even with the inadequacies and paradoxes in these studies, the data
seem to strengthen the deterrence interpretation for the effect of the law of
12 July 1978. The French law seems to have been effective because of its

advertised and notorious threat of sanctions. The drinking driver could be deterred by legal threats even in the wine-centered culture of France. However, as in the United Kingdom, the deterrent effectiveness of the Scandinavian-type law proved to be evanescent. My proposed explanation is similar to that offered for the U.K. case: The actual chance of detection and punishment was negligible, as the driving population learned through experience.

The risk of being tested for blood alcohol under the 1978 law in France was very low, and the probability of the test's being defined as positive was incredibly small. Between the inception of the new law and the end of January 1979, fewer than 1,100 roadblocks were authorized in all of France. Only 1,416 positive results were recorded out of more than 335,000 tests given, a fraction of less than half of 1 percent. This finding is on its face incredible, even if the true fraction of alcohol-impaired drivers was the 1.8 percent cited in the postlaw ONSER study, and if the police did not concentrate their roadblocks at times and places where drinking drivers were especially common (recall further that the police Alcotests were calibrated at the low level of 0.5 pro mille).

My experience in viewing the French police in action suggests that both the rarity of tests and the low frequency of positive results were due to official diffidence in enforcing the legislation. As noted in an interview with a high police official, the public failed to understand and resented the police function in the general area of traffic law, and the police had difficulty in relating to this unfamiliar type of lawbreaker: "We would much rather chase bandits than speeders."

In sum, if the initial publicity and subsequent quarrels concerning the law of 12 July 1978 had produced the impression of a certain, severe, and prompt punishment for drinking drivers, the everyday experience of drivers on the French highways did not reinforce this impression. In the words of a lawyer specializing in the defense of traffic-law violators, the public discovered the official threat to be a "wooden shoe"—perhaps the French equivalent of a "paper tiger."

The Netherlands

The Netherlands law of 1 November 1974 is unusual among recent adoptions of the Scandinavian approach to drinking and driving in that it is more closely modeled on the 1936 Norwegian law than on the British Road Safety Act. The level of tolerance for blood alcohol in the Dutch law is 50 milligrams/100 milliliters, the same as in Norway and relatively low by world standards. The penalties are relatively high, including fines of up to f5,000 (more than U.S. $2,000), license suspensions of up to five years, and prison terms of up to three months. Although no data have been reported concerning the financial and license penalties meted out in practice, under the prior law it was reported that unconditional prison sentences were routine for violations in the western, most populated, part of the Netherlands.

The law provides for screening breath tests with a device calibrated at 50 milligrams/100 milliliters, but unlike in the United Kingdom, the Dutch police must always have reason to suspect a driver of having consumed alcohol before they can administer the test. The police participate in roadblocks in the Norwegian manner; only if they smell alcohol on the breath may the screening test be demanded. Suspects failing the screening test in the field are required to take a second test at the police station, this one calibrated at 80 milligrams. A peculiar feature of Dutch law is that a driver failing the first test but passing the second is not prosecuted (although he may be violating the law); however, he is prohibited from driving until his blood-alcohol concentration falls below the legal limit. Only a driver failing both screening tests is required to give a blood sample for analysis, which if positive, results in prosecution (Noordzij 1977; SWOV 1977).

It is reported that the law was introduced with extensive publicity (Noordzij 1977, p. 454), as was fitting for this relatively complicated legislation. Following passage of the law, prosecutions for drinking and driving rose, more than doubling—to about 20,000 per year—in the first full year.

A research team from the Netherlands Institute for Road Safety Research (SWOV) had been gathering blood-alcohol-concentration data from a national sample of sites on weekend nights by means of roadside surveys in 1970, 1971, and 1973 (the 1973 sampling was terminated at the time of the fuel crisis). With the anticipated inception of the law of 1974, surveys were put into the field beginning the weekend prior to the change and again two weeks and four weeks later. Roadside surveys also were made by a slightly different, though comparable, method in 1975.

The basic results of SWOV's evaluation are presented in figure 4-8 which shows the presence and levels of blood-alcohol concentrations in samples between 1970 and 1975. Surprisingly, the figure does not differentiate the 1974 survey data before and after the legal change, and the accompanying text indicates that the decrease appeared in the October survey as well as the November one. The difference between the years is striking and is in the direction predicted by the deterrence model. The 1975 data seem to show some continued but weakening effect of the law, and a small residual effect is claimed as late as 1979 (Noordzij 1980). The refusal rate in these surveys ranged up to 18 percent, but perhaps because drivers confused the survey with the expected police operations refusals were only 3 percent in the crucial 1974 sounding. Assuming that refusals were more likely to be

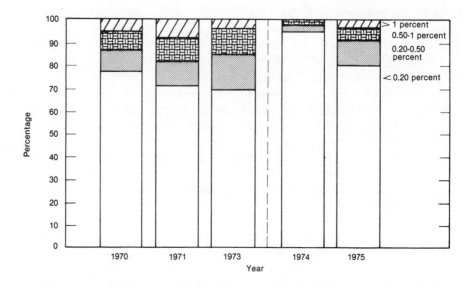

Source: Noordzij 1977, p. 457. Reprinted by permission of the Australian Governmental Publishing Service.
Figure 4-8. Blood-Alcohol Distributions from Roadside Surveys in the Netherlands

from people having consumed alcohol, the differences in figure 4-8 are expressed conservatively. (With full cooperation, additional elevated blood-alcohol concentrations would be found most often in those years when the survey met greatest resistance and least often in 1973.)

Unfortunately, the clear picture presented in figure 4-8 is complicated by the failure to find comparable effects in the curve of fatalities, shown in figure 4-9, which is completely dominated by the decline associated with the 1973 oil crisis. Better support for deterrence-based expectations is found in the curves of nighttime accidents (figure 4-10) and of weekend crashes (figure 4-11), although an inquiry into nighttime fatal crashes found no changes in the ratio of single- to multiple-vehicle crashes, which is usually a good measure of alcohol involvement. Statistics on crashes judged to be alcohol involved support expectations, but as the reader knows, I counsel against using such data since they depend on unreliable police judgments.

Although the evidence is not uniformly favorable, Noordzij has concluded that the new law was effective, reducing fatal crashes by 100 (or 35 percent) for the initial year and reducing total crashes by 5 percent (1977, p. 40). If these estimates are correct, and if the relationship between alcohol and crashes is similar in the Netherlands to that demonstrated in

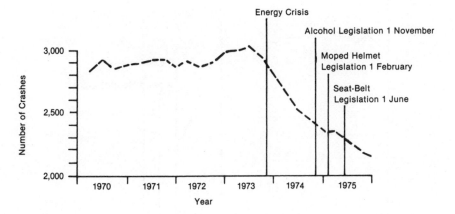

Source: Noordzij 1977, p. 466. Reprinted by permission of the Australian Governmental Publishing Service.
Figure 4-9. Total Fatal Crashes (Twelve-Month Moving Average) in the Netherlands

other countries, the Dutch law has been nearly perfectly effective in eliminating the contribution of alcohol to highway crashes.

I would be more guarded in interpreting these data. The time series of roadside surveys is impressive, but it does not control for history, and the critical year of 1974 is also the one that follows the fuel crisis. Quite likely, in 1974, the greater cost and lower availability of fuel had an independent effect, reducing driving associated with drinking. For instance, people may have been less likely to drive when going out for an evening's recreation. The fact that the decline in blood-alcohol concentrations was perceived even before the law's inception also would be compatible with an explanation involving the fuel crisis. Furthermore, the lack of confirmation of deterrence expectations in crash-related fatalities is disappointing. Although Noordzij may have been right in claiming some deterrent effectiveness for the Dutch legislation, I strongly doubt that the law produced as large an effect as he estimated.

The conclusion of a deterrent effect for the Dutch law is indicated in a study, reported by the Rotterdam police (Van Ooijen 1977), of alcohol-related crashes resulting in injury. Although the time-series curve in this study beautifully supports the conclusion of deterrent effectiveness, I feel that relatively little confidence should be placed in these data because of their basis in subjective judgments concerning alcohol involvement. These judgments repeatedly have been shown to be incorrect when compared to objective data from chemical tests (Coldwell 1957).

In sum, the study of the Netherlands law potentially is of great interest because of the stringency of the legislation and the availability of survey-

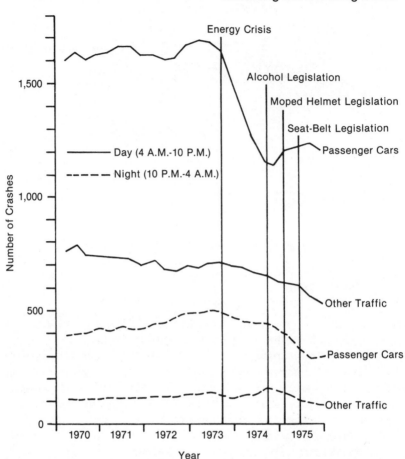

Source: Noordzij 1977, p. 467. Reprinted by permission of the Australian Governmental Publishing Service.

Figure 4-10. Fatal Crashes, by Type of Vehicle and Time of Day (Twelve-Month Moving Average) in the Netherlands

based data on blood-alcohol concentrations among non-crash-involved drivers. However, the unfortunate timing of the legislation from the viewpoint of evaluation and the use of methodology that fails to control for history make the demonstration of changes in levels of blood alcohol among Dutch drivers rather ambiguous evidence for the deterrence model. The observed changes in the survey-based data can be explained by responses to the fuel crisis. The failure of these changes to be reflected in crash-based data series threatens the deterrence interpretation offered by

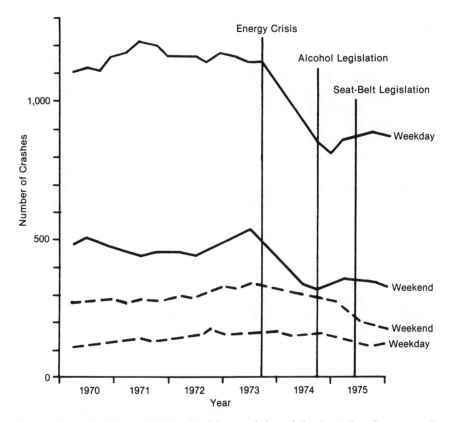

Source: Noordzij 1977, p. 468. Reprinted by permission of the Australian Governmental Publishing Service.

Figure 4-11. Fatal Crashes Involving Passenger Cars, by Day and Time of Day (Twelve-Month Moving Average) in the Netherlands

Noordzij. In light of its conformity to expectations generated by theory and confirmed in similar cases elsewhere, it is not necessary to discard the deterrence interpretation of this case completely, but its assertion must be tentative and guarded.

The Netherlands case also shows the now familiar return of a depressed curve of casualties to normal over a relatively short time. To the extent that the depression was due to the fuel crisis, the subsequent return of plentiful oil supplies (even though at higher prices) is an appealing explanation. To the extent that the depression was due to law-based deterrence, the evanescent nature of deterrent effects due to Scandinavian-type laws concerning drinking and driving is again demonstrated.

Canada

The Canadian "Breathaliser" legislation followed closely, in both timing and form, the British Road Safety Act of 1967. It has been evaluated independently by two different teams, both of which reached the conclusion that the Canadian law had a moderate but temporary and evanescent effect on the drinking-and-driving problem (Carr, Goldberg, and Farbar 1974, 1975; Chambers, Roberts, and Voeller 1976).

Canadian policy on drinking and driving is controlled by federal legislation affecting all the provinces. The Scandinavian model was adopted in the Canadian Criminal Law Amendment Act that took effect on 1 December 1969. The legislation and subsequent official evaluation reflect a belief in the effectiveness of the 1967 British law. However, at least in retrospect, several important provisions differentiate the Canadian law from its U.K. forerunner.

The heart of the Canadian legislation is the empowering of police officers to require breath tests based on "reasonable and probable" grounds to believe that a driver is impaired by alcohol. As in the United Kingdom, the tolerated blood-alcohol concentration is 0.08 percent. The breath test is mandatory, refusal being punished by fines and imprisonment identical to penalties for failing the test. The breath test is a quantitative and evidentiary one, not requiring a subsequent blood test, but in practice requiring the use of stationary testing equipment at police stations instead of portable equipment in patrol vehicles, as in the United Kingdom. Penalties for failing the breath test include fines up to $1,000 and/or prison for up to six months. License suspension originally was at the discretion of the court, although this was changed to mandatory suspension following a 1973 Supreme Court decision. Neither published evaluation of the Canadian legislation provides information on actual fines and jail sentences or on license suspensions following convictions of drinking drivers.

The first analysis of the results of this legislation (Carr, Goldberg, and Farbar 1974) was based largely on reported crashes through 1971. Data were presented separately for injury-producing crashes and for fatal crashes, and they were analyzed both for the province of Ontario separately, and for the country as a whole. The national data on fatal crashes are presented in figure 4-12. Their form, though not the statistical analysis, follows the interrupted time-series model. One may reasonably conclude from inspection of the figure that fatalities responded to the Canadian legislation. The report's conclusions are positive but guarded:

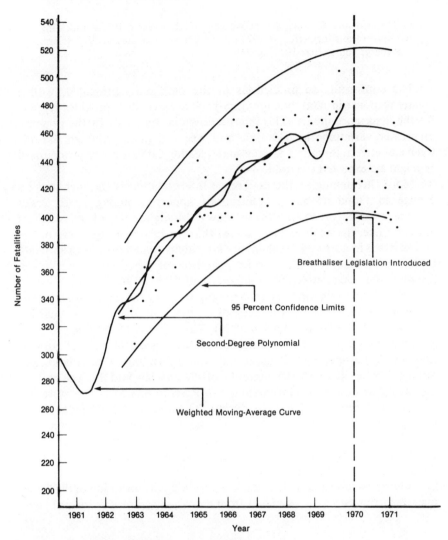

Source: Carr, Goldberg, and Farbar 1975, figure 2.2.

Figure 4-12. Crash-Related Fatalities in Canada, Seasonally Adjusted

All four figures show a significant number of points below the trend line . . . indicating that serious accidents have undergone a statistically significant decline, relative to the trend, since the introduction of the Breathaliser Legislation. In fact, for victims killed in Canada, the average monthly post-Breathaliser figures are 9 percent below the trend.

[F]atal accidents in the United States [offered as a control] decreased by about 2.1 percent from 1969 to 1970 while comparable figures for Canada show a decrease of 6.3 percent. It may also be noticed that injury accidents in Ontario and Canada are above the trend in early 1971—indicating possibly a transitory effect in 1970 that may have dissipated in 1971. [Carr, Goldberg, and Farbar 1974, p. 24]

The conformity to predictions of the time series presented, with a greater response in fatal than in injury-producing crashes, provides support for the deterrence model. This interpretation is confirmed by the presence of greater variations in nighttime and weekend data, although the differences between these and daytime and weekday data are not as pronounced as might be expected (see table 4-3).

More threatening to the deterrence interpretation is the fact that no change in blood-alcohol concentrations appeared among tested crash fatalities from before to after the new law. Although testing of cadavers was not complete, the analysts have denied that the incompleteness was major or that it was important in explaining the findings, which remain an anomaly in this otherwise convincing documentation of deterrent effects for a Scandinavian-type law (Carr, Goldberg, and Farbar 1974, p. 105).

The second evaluation, by epidemiologists using the same data base but somewhat different analytical methods, is more positive and less guarded (Chambers, Roberts, and Voeller 1976). The analysts found that the total incidence rate (for crash-related deaths and injuries on the basis of population at risk) declined by 9.2 deaths and injuries per 100,000 population per quarter during the first fifteen months of the new law and that the bulk of the saving was during nighttime hours (6 P.M. to 6 A.M.). The mortality rate was reduced by 7.7 percent during the same period. Changes in the form of reporting during 1971 cut off the possiblility of computing the nighttime-to-daytime crash ratio after the period mentioned. However, the epidemiologists agreed with previous analysts that the deterrent effects of the legislation were of short duration.

Additional information is available concerning the operation of the Canadian law from survey research and from a quasi-experimental study of some

Table 4-3
Fatal and Serious-Injury Crashes in Canada in 1970 Compared with 1969

Period	Changes in Fatal Crashes	Changes in Fatal and Injury Crashes
Night: 10 P.M. to 4 A.M.	− 10%	− 5.8%
Day: 4 A.M. to 10 P.M.	− 8%	+ 1.4%
Weekends: Friday to Sunday	− 10%	− 1.3%
Weekdays: Monday to Thursday	− 6%	+ 1.3%

Source: Carr et al. 1974, p. 97. No tests of significance are provided.

arbitrarily selected Toronto drinking places. A large-scale national survey was commissioned, with waves before and after inception of the new law, to determine public knowledge. The survey showed that even before a publicity campaign was launched the law was well known; subsequently, it was recognized by nearly everyone. Almost all drivers surveyed knew that, in accordance with the terms of the new law, police could give breath tests. Drivers also knew that license suspension was a possible consequence of conviction for drinking and driving (Kates, Peat, Marwick 1970).

The Toronto study (Smart 1972) included counts of cars in parking lots of four suburban taverns early in the evening (6 P.M.) and later (10 P.M.) during the three months prior to and three months subsequent to the new law. A sharp decline in the number of cars was noted during the first month of the new law (December 1969). This decline continued through February 1970 for the later hours, but it diminished for the earlier hours. No change was found in the average number of occupants in the vehicles or in the observed alcohol consumption of those who patronized the taverns. However, the methodology failed to control for history; it made no correction for possible seasonal variations that might explain a decline in patronage at the beginning of December and in February without deterrence. The observer's unsystematic impression on 2 December is perhaps better and more-persuasive evidence for the deterrent effect of the Canadian law than the quantitative data from the study:

> To anyone observing tavern parking lots on the day after the new Canadian law came into force its effects could scarcely be doubted. Parking lots were nearly empty for the first time in three months. [Smart 1972, p. 1126]

Although some deterrent effect for the Canadian legislation is usually conceded, the consensus is that it was less marked and less prolonged than the effect of the British Road Safety Act of 1967, after which the Canadian law was patterned. Three categories of reasons for these differences have been suggested, and I cannot disagree with them. First, the actual threat posed by the law was less in Canada than in the United Kingdom. Police were not empowered to test a motorist's breath merely because he was in an accident or had committed a traffic-law violation, as in the United Kingdom. Moreover, police cars did not carry testing devices, and the demand of a test thus was more difficult and perhaps less likely to be made than in the United Kingdom. Also, license suspension in Canada was originally left to the discretion of the court, rather than being mandatory as in the United Kingdom (Carr and his associates erroneously asserted that license suspension was at the discretion of the court in both countries).

Second, the threat posed by the Canadian law does not appear to have been publicized as well as that of the British law. Although the Canadian law was well known, the legislation was not considered particularly controversial or newsworthy, and publicity about it did not necessarily encourage fear of apprehension.

Third, the actual probability of apprehension and conviction for drinking and driving in Canada apparently was negligible both before and after the new law. An observer writing in 1977 noted that, according to official estimates, there were 26,000 kilometers of impaired driving for every drinking-and-driving charge in Canada:

> Detection procedures are such that only the worst cases are likely to catch the attention of police. [Detection is] really a chance event. [Ennis 1977, p. 19]

In summary, the Criminal Law Amendment Act of 1969 in Canada, although modeled on the prior British legislation, was in fact as well as perception less threatening; its penalties were less severe and its enforcement more difficult for the police. Under these circumstances, the Canadian law might well be expected to have had a smaller effect than the British law, and this expectation is supported in the reported evaluative studies. Moreover, as in the previous cases studied, the deterrent effect in Canada appears to have been evanescent. This is understandable given the very low certainty of punishment experienced by Canadian drivers, who may have learned over time to discount a threat that experience teaches is in fact negligible.

New Zealand

New Zealand's legislative history in the matter of drinking and driving closely followed the model of the British Road Safety Act. In New Zealand, the Transport Amendment Act of 1966 had established a procedure for taking blood samples of accused drivers. In 1969, following the U.K. example, the status of a blood-alcohol concentration of 100 milligrams/100 milliliters was changed from a rebuttable presumption of alcoholic influence to an absolute limit, and cooperation in furnishing blood samples was made compulsory. Although other modifications of the law in the direction of the Scandinavian approach subsequently took place, the 1969 change is considered the most substantial and has furnished the basis of the principal published evaluation of the New Zealand law (Hurst 1978).

The 1969 compulsory-blood-test law provided that a police officer could demand a screening breath test of a driver if the officer had "good cause to suspect an alcohol offense" (Hurst 1978, p. 228) (in 1974, it became necessary only to suspect the driver of having consumed alcohol). Failure of the initial test led to a second test twenty minutes later. Failure of

the second breath test resulted in the requirement of a blood test. Cooperation with the screening tests was not mandatory, but noncompliance
rendered the blood test compulsory. Refusal of the blood test led to the
same penalties as failure of the test. These penalties included a minimum
license suspension (disqualification) of six months, except in "special circumstances," in addition to fines and possible prison (detention). Typical
sentences since the 1969 law have been fines of $50 to $400 and license
suspensions averaging twelve months.

In the first full year under the new law, there were nearly 5,000
drinking-and-driving prosecutions in New Zealand, a rate approximately
three times that in England and Wales under the Road Safety Act (based on
vehicle registrations). By 1975, the rate had more than doubled, after which
it stayed relatively constant. Furthermore, the proportion of prosecutions
ending in convictions reached between 96 and 97 percent.

Hurst's evaluation of the New Zealand legislation used a variety of official measures of effect. His overall conclusion was negative:

> It is concluded that the 1969 law did not have the kind of immediate effect
> that was achieved in Great Britain in 1967. There may have been a more
> gradual effect, but one cannot be confident that such an effect occurred.
> The difference in impact was almost certainly due to attendant cir-
> cumstances and the quite different types of publicity given the alcohol cam-
> paigns in the two countries. It was clearly not attributable to differences in
> the statute's content or in its enforcement, which has always been relatively
> active and has increased over the years. [1978, p. 287]

This negative conclusion seems to be overly pessimistic. I believe it
results in part from reliance on inappropriate data—police estimates of
alcohol involvement, for example, which are an inadequate basis for scientific evaluations—and in part from Hurst's anticipation of larger and more-
permanent results than were warranted from the nature of the law.

I interpret the small changes in the data series as supporting the conclusion that New Zealand's drinking-and-driving law did have an immediate
deterrent effect on the problem, although not a lasting one. The data are
not sufficiently precise to render a firm or dependable basis for estimating
the effect, and it is not possible to quarrel with Hurst on statistical grounds.
However, this umpire would call the game differently.

The first criterion used by Hurst is "reported alcohol involvement in accidents." This takes the form of only very brief time series, because data
from before 1968 were not available and because the manner of reporting
crashes changed radically eight months after the change in the drinking-
and-driving law. Hurst found that the proportion of reported alcohol-
involved fatal crashes went from 23 percent in 1968 to 21 percent in the first
four months of 1969 (before the change in the law) and then to 25 percent in

the balance of 1969. Reported alcohol involvement in injury crashes was 8 percent, 12 percent, and 11 percent respectively in the three time periods. Clearly, these changes are small, very likely nonsignificant, and in the case of fatal accidents, unfavorable to the deterrence interpretation. However, for reasons presented in the methodological discussion (chapter 3), police reports concerning alcohol involvement are not scientifically acceptable. I would place little weight on the negative conclusions drawn from these data.

Data on fatal crashes in New Zealand are available for a more-extended period and are reported on an annual basis from 1968 through 1973 (they are reported separately during 1969 before and after the legal change). These data appear as the upper dashed line in figure 4-13. There was a 6 percent decline in fatal crashes during the postintervention period of 1969. Hurst acknowledged this change but noted that "the numbers involved are too small to prove that anything beyond chance was operating" (p. 289). Nonfatal crashes, diagramed in the top line of figure 4-13, did not decrease, but the increase in the postintervention period was the smallest in the series. Again, Hurst pointed to the nonsignificance of the change. Nighttime fatal crashes, the bottom line in the figure, dipped proportionately even more; indeed, the decline in total fatal crashes is entirely explained by the nighttime decline.

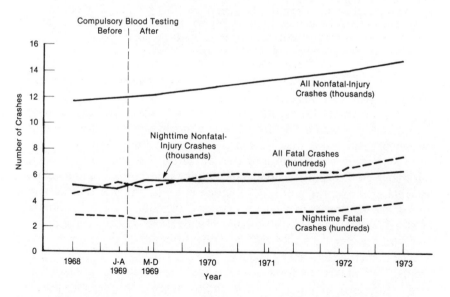

Source: Hurst 1978, p. 290. Reprinted with permission from *Accident Analysis and Prevention*, vol. 10, R.M. Hurst, "Blood Test Legislation in New Zealand," Copyright 1978, Pergamon Press, Ltd.

Figure 4-13. Fatal and Injury-Producing Crashes in New Zealand

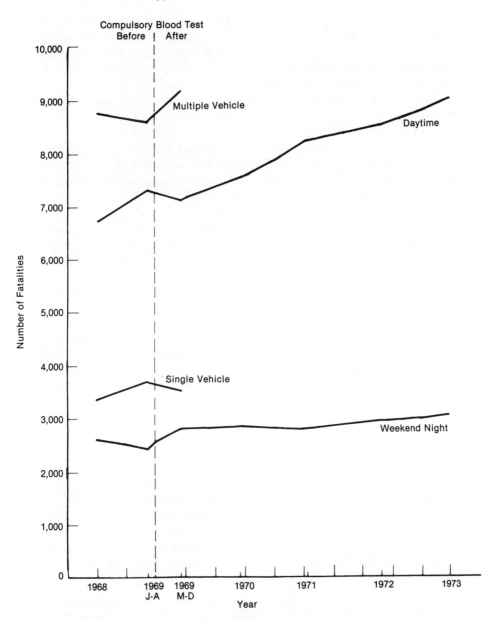

Source: Hurst 1978, p. 291. Reprinted with permission from *Accident Analysis and Prevention*, vol. 10, R.M. Hurst, "Blood Test Legislation in New Zealand," Copyright 1978, Pergamon Press, Ltd.

Figure 4-14. Fatal and Injury-Producing Crashes in New Zealand, by Time and Type

Additional relevant data appear in figure 4-14. Weekend crashes (combining fatal and nonfatal) did not vary as suggested by theoretical expectations. However, three-point series of single-vehicle and multiple-vehicle crashes did conform to expectations based on the hypothesis that alcohol involvement in crashes was reduced by the legal change (alcohol is more often involved in single-vehicle crashes, and this series behaves in the predicted manner). Again, without a basis for estimating random variation, Hurst was correct in concluding that statistical significance is lacking.

The official New Zealand data, as presented here, are far from ideal measures of the effect of the 1969 law. The series are very short, and although several years are covered, in most of these years the absence of monthly breakdowns severely limits the number of observation points. Nonetheless, three of the four comparisons, although not statistically significant, do support expectations based on the deterrence model. On the one hand, if a deep and long effect of the law was expected, then the results must be considered disappointing. On the other hand, if a 6 percent decline in fatal crashes is meaningful and if expectations include a possible return of matters to the status quo ante in a relatively short time, the New Zealand experience is arguably one that is at least consistent with the deterrence model.

It is possible that monthly data pertaining to the series presented by Hurst yet may be available and that further analysis of the series based on these data may provide more support for an effect of the law than his analysis yields. In the absence of such data, the deterrence interpretation seems as reasonable as that of little or no effect, and it is in accord with experience in most other situations examined in this report. If the curve of fatal crashes in figure 4-13 is matched with the comparable one from the United Kingdom in figure 4-2, the difference between the U.K. and New Zealand experiences does not seem fundamental. New Zealand data were not adequate to attempt a replication of figure 4-3, which so conclusively supports the attainment of deterrence in the U.K. case.

It is worthwhile noting that the New Zealand law was not favored with publicity as strong as the publicity that apparently helped the British law create the impression of punishment for violators. The New Zealand publicity is not described in detail in Hurst's article, but the discussion section notes that:

> [P]ublicity emphasized social values and the need to reduce the accident risk from drinking. There was no great attempt to frighten potential offenders, and the "due cause to suspect" provision was not only explained but advertised. It may be that these efforts toward public enlightenment blunted the edge of the law. [1978, pp. 295-296]

Furthermore, the 1969 New Zealand law does not appear to have been a matter of national news, as was the British Road Safety Act of 1967.

Hurst suggested that a second reason for the "failure of New Zealand to match the British experience" lies in the greater novelty of the alcohol-testing provisions in the British law. He was mistaken on this point; the United Kingdom, like New Zealand, had blood-test provisions in its earlier law—the Road Traffic Act of 1962—and the relative novelty of the two legal changes strikes me as about the same.

The most bothersome problem in assimilating the New Zealand experience and the Scandinavian approach in other countries is the failure of weekend-night fatalities to accord with expectations. In fact, they vary in the wrong direction and I am unable to explain this. If this point can be overlooked, the results are in keeping with what one might expect for a deterrence-based law that suffered from inadequate publicity and newsworthiness. Small responses in some data series that can indicate changes in drinking and driving were found, although the size of these variations and the aggregation of data do not suffice to render them statistically significant. If these are more than chance variations, it may be the case that the New Zealand law produced a moderate, short-term-deterrent effect. It is difficult to say more on the positive side; what cannot be said is that the New Zealand experience casts doubt on the ability of the Scandinavian approach to deter drinking and driving in the short run.

Australia

Perhaps the earliest important adoption of the Scandinavian approach abroad occurred in the Australian state of Victoria in 1966, the year before the United Kingdom enacted its Road Safety Act. Discussion of the Australian legislation has been left to this point because the law was introduced under such unfavorable conditions for both effectiveness and scientific analysis that little confidence can be placed in the sole evaluative report, which is on its face unfavorable to deterrence theory.

Victorian drinking-and-driving law began to evolve from the classical model toward the Scandinavian in 1958 with the provision for blood samples given voluntarily by the accused, taken with the aid of a private physician, and usable in prosecution only as part of the total evidentiary package. There would seem to have been little incentive for the accused to cooperate with this procedure. In 1961, an evidentiary breath test was substituted for the blood test, and in the following year it was made compulsory, although originally there was only a small fine for refusers (the circumstances under which it could be requested are not mentioned in the literature).

The Scandinavian approach was more fully adopted in Victoria in 1966, following the recommendation of a Royal Commission studying drinking and driving, when the law was modified to prohibit driving with a blood-alcohol concentration of more than 0.05 percent. The details of this law are not clear in the sparse literature. One commentator has stated that the penalty for violation was extraordinarily low—a fine of not more than $100 (Jamieson 1968). Moreover, the law "received publicity but was not accorded any public education program by the authorities" (Birrell 1975, p. 777). No mention is made in the literature of the new law's being controversial or newsworthy, which is surprising in light of its pioneering nature and the appointment of a Royal Commission in the matter.

Thus, the introduction of the 1966 law in Victoria seems to have been affected by low severity of penalties and low visibility. The numbers of breath tests did increase—from 1,218 in 1961; to 4,178 in 1967; to 10,793 in 1972—although even the latter figures may be viewed as consistent with a very low risk of apprehension for the drinking driver.

Unfortunately, the only published evaluation of the Victorian legislation is contained in a conference paper by a police physician whose principal interest seems to have been in descriptive studies of the distribution of blood-alcohol concentrations. The author, concluding that there was no impact, failed to present data on the basis of which an independent assessment could be made (Birrell 1975).

Any attempt to evaluate the deterrence-based provisions of the Victorian law of 1966 would indeed face difficulties, because the enacting legislation included the simultaneous adoption of a change in the closing hours of pubs from 6 P.M. to 10 P.M. Birrell reported merely that "there was a quite remarkable shift in the times of occurrence of serious traffic accidents but virtually no change in the total number of crashes and deaths" (p. 777). Given the modest penalties that compromised perceived severity, and the lack of publicity or newsworthiness that compromised perceived certainty, it would have been unreasonable to expect marked deterrent effectiveness from the law, even if the methodological problems posed by the simultaneous enactment of changed closing hours could have been overcome. The conclusion on the Victorian law of 1966, then, must be that no effects were demonstrated but that the deterrence model was so poorly complied with as to render unrealistic any expectations of change.

Other Countries

The research literature mentions adoptions of drinking-and-driving laws modeled on the Scandinavian ones, with attempts at evaluation, in Austria and Czechoslovakia in 1961 and in Germany in 1966 and 1973. However, the reports are so sketchy that the results are only marginally enlightening. The available information is summarized here.

What seems to have been a per se law was adopted in Austria, effective 1 January 1961. At an international conference the following year, it was reported that crashes had diminished (Breitenecker 1962). Between 1960 and 1961 accidents were reduced by 26 percent, injuries by 28 percent, and deaths by 16 percent. Between 1961 and the first six months of 1962, accidents were reported to have been reduced by 10 percent, injuries by 18 percent, and deaths by 26 percent. If the contribution of alcohol to deaths, injuries, and total crashes in Austria is at all like that in other countries, these reductions are extremely high. However, as noted by Breitenecker:

> [A]fter some months there was a rise in traffic accidents. But the incidence of fatal accidents did not reach the peak to which it had climbed before the introduction of the new act. The limit of 0.8 pro mille had proved its worth from the outset, but statistical proof is faced with numerous external obstacles. [1962, p. 336]

Unfortunately, this report presented no information on the previous law, the origin of the reform, the provisions other than the 0.8 pro mille (0.08 percent) limit, or the manner of application. Lacking this information one can say little other than that, in Austria as in many other countries, a law with the intent to deter drinking and driving was followed by an initial drop in casualty measures and a subsequent rise toward the status quo ante.

It is reported that Czechoslovakia also changed its drinking-and-driving legislation on 1 January 1961. "The consumption of alcohol has been forbidden for all drivers" (SWOV 1969, p. 36). Unfortunately, even less is reported about this innovation than about the Austrian one. Official crash statistics from the Czech Ministry of Interior are noted, but these seem to show no inflection corresponding to the legislative reform. The percentage of crashes represented as "alcohol accidents" did decline in 1961, and it remained at a reduced level, but in the absence of a definition of this term, I suspect that it refers to police judgments of alcohol influence, which should not be considered acceptable evidence of the law's effectiveness.

A manuscript concerning the German literature on alcohol and traffic mentions several changes in the drinking-and-driving law (Vogt 1980). Drinking and driving was first criminalized in 1952. A maximum tolerated blood-alcohol concentration of 0.15 percent was specified in 1953 but without a prescribed level of punishment. In 1966, the level of toleration was lowered to 0.13 percent, and the commentator noted:

> There has been a major change in the yearly rate of drunk driving cases. . . . In respect to severe accidents in which drunk drivers were involved, the rate decreased after 1967. [Vogt 1980]

The accompanying data are of declining convictions, which do not furnish a suitable criterion for evaluating the role of alcohol in crashes. Indeed, the legislation would look more succesful with an increase in convictions, suggesting realism for the legal threat. A decrease in convictions could indicate, for example, merely a shift in enforcement resources or a lowering of findings of guilt among those charged with the offense of drinking and driving.

Another legal change in 1973 lowered the level of toleration to 0.08 percent and provided for loss of the driver's license for a month on conviction. The accompanying evaluative data concerning this change are figures of drivers "causing injury in accidents" for twenty-four months surrounding the inception of the law. Again, the data may be inadequate to test the deterrence model. Vogt (1980) concluded that "the new law influenced drinking-and-driving for only a very short time period." This conclusion is in keeping with expectations based on experience in other countries.

Norway and Sweden

Discussion of the simple deterrent effects of the original Scandinavian laws has been postponed to the end of this chapter because the scientifically acceptable evidence is ambiguous. The interrupted time-series methodology, which has yielded a relatively consistent pattern of evidence for the ability of the Scandinavian approach to deter drinking and driving in the short run, fails to detect comparable results when applied to data from Norway and Sweden.

In light of the consistency of findings from other jurisdictions, I believe that the application of this method to the Scandinavian data must be closely scrutinized for its appropriateness and that a wide net should be spread to gather together other relevant evidence about the Scandinavian experience. These endeavors have led me to the conclusion that the 1936 law in Norway and the 1941 law in Sweden, although they serve to define the Scandinavian approach to drinking and driving, probably achieved little marginal deterrence. However, both laws must be viewed as relatively small increments in the development of the overall Scandinavian approach, which may in sum have achieved a general preventive effect because of the duration and consistency of the efforts involved.

Unfortunately, scientifically convincing demonstration of the long-range accomplishments of Swedish and Norwegian drinking-and-driving laws is extremely difficult because of many plausible rival explanations. In the first place, although it can be shown that drinking and driving in some of its manifestations is less common in Norway and Sweden than in, say, Canada or the United States, it cannot be similarly demonstrated that the level is lower than it was in Scandinavia before mounting the legal effort or lower than during the early stages of the effort. In the second place, even if this were demonstrated, other differences between these countries and those compared in the culture of alcohol and the automobile, including other legal efforts such as controls on the distribution of drink, might partly or even completely explain the Scandinavian experience in this area. Review of the broader evidence, aided in large part by the efforts of Johannes Andenaes (1978) and John R. Snortum (1981), persuades me that the deterrence-based legal approach taken as a whole may have had long-range general preventive effects in Norway and Sweden, despite the failure of the laws of 1936 and 1941 to produce measurable increments in deterrence. However, I do not believe that this achievement, if confirmed, justifies the wisdom of all steps taken in its behalf. In particular, the deterrent achievements concerning drinking and driving in other countries suggest to me that punishments such as mandatory prison are very likely unnecessary. I am also skeptical that demonstration of general preventive results in Norway and Sweden can serve to justify the adoption of comparable measures in other countries where the cultural definitions of alcohol and automobiles may sharply diverge from the Scandinavian definition.

The time series indicating drinking and driving in the Scandinavian countries are presented in figures 4-15 and 4-16. These refer to fatal crashes in Sweden and to crash-related fatalities in Norway. Unlike the majority of cases reviewed in this chapter, the time series in Norway and Sweden pro-

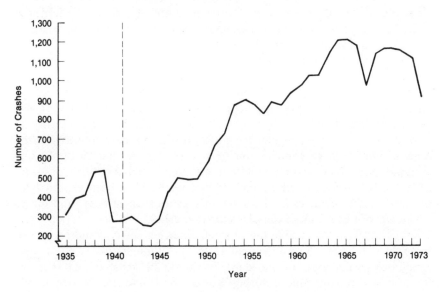

Source: Ross 1975, p. 300. Copyright by The University of Chicago Press. Reprinted with permission.

Figure 4-15. Fatal Crashes in Sweden

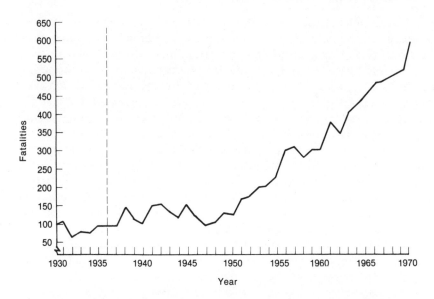

Figure 4-16. Motor-Vehicle Fatalities in Norway

vide no evidence to support expectations of simple deterrence. Indeed, the immediate response of fatal crashes and fatalities to the new laws seems to have been, if anything, in the wrong direction.

For several reasons, the reader should not rush to the conclusion that the deterrence-based claims for the Scandinavian laws have been disproved. First, the series used were crude surrogates for drinking and driving; more-refined series such as weekend-night and single-vehicle crashes were not available this early in the history of the automobile and of social statistics. Furthermore, to the extent that the crash problem in these countries at the time involved a large contribution from causes other than alcohol—for-example, poor roads and a population unsophisticated about driving—successful deterrence of drinking and driving would have been expected to-produce smaller changes in the index of crashes than in times and places where alcohol was a large causal factor in crashes.

Second, it is conceivable that a small deterrent effect could have been overridden by chance or historical factors. Although this is not a parsimonious explanation of the data, it should be remembered that the Swedish law was introduced during World War II and the Norwegian one deep in the Great Depression.

The most important caution to be observed in interpreting these data is that the interrupted time-series methodology assumes one is studying a sharp change in the causal variable that would, under theoretical expectations, very likely produce a sharp change in the effect. The more-recent adoptions of the Scandinavian approach usually fit the model well, but this appears not to have been the case for the Norwegian and Swedish laws. Although in retrospect these laws clearly and fundamentally redefined the drinking-and-driving offense, they were adopted in legal systems that already had license suspensions and prison sentences for drinking drivers and that already used medical examinations including blood tests in processing those accused of drinking and driving. Also important from the viewpoint of the deterrence model is the following information:

> In striking contrast to what occurred in England in 1967, little publicity was given to the [Norwegian] Act of 1936 and its coming into force. During the passage of the Bill through the Storting, the spokesman concerned expressed surprise over the fact that there had not been more discussion of the matter in the press, although a step was now being taken that had no precedent in the legislation of any country. And a perusal of the country's two leading motoring journals of the period . . . yields the surprising result that neither the Act nor the practice to which it gave rise are mentioned at all either in 1936 or 1937. It is possible that knowledge of the law and the practice only gradually percolated through to drivers. [Andenaes 1978, pp. 41-42][a]

In summary, it may well be an error to treat the Norwegian law of 1936 and the Swedish one of 1941 as interventions comparable in nature, and therefore in potential impact, to the British Road Safety Act. Since the increments in actual certainty, severity, and celerity of punishment were much smaller, and the publicity and newsworthiness much less, it would be unreasonable to have expected a large impact from these interventions. In addition, the role of alcohol in crashes at these times and places very likely was less pronounced due to the higher relative contributions of other factors. The laws were introduced at a time when other historical events may have been strongly influencing crashes, and the measures of the effect variables were relatively insensitive. Therefore, it would not have been surprising to find little evidence for deterrence in the time series. Had the results been positive, they would have produced considerable support for the deterrent effectiveness of the Scandinavian approach to drinking and driving. However, the negative results are not as disastrous as they might seem at first glance, given all the conditions noted.

Since the interrupted time-series method yields little enlightenment concerning the Norwegian and Swedish laws, it is appropriate to search for other sources of evidence. During the visit to Scandinavia, and subsequently, I tried to accumulate evidence that originators and supporters of the deterrence approach offered in support of their claims. This job has

---

[a]Reprinted with permission.

now been perhaps better performed by Snortum (1981). Although Snortum views the evidence more positively then I, we seem to recognize the same arguments and data, which are summarized next.

Perhaps the most commonly heard argument in support of the deterrent effectiveness of the Scandinavian laws involves testimony from residents and visitors based on introspection and unsystematic observation. People are said to be aware of the law and to fear its threat. The stereotypical anecdote concerns parties at which great quantities of liquor are consumed by all present except drivers (a role often said to be occupied by wives, even in these reputedly egalitarian societies). Although one hesitates to doubt the anecdotes, I find that they provide no scientifically acceptable evidence for the proposition they illustrate. Johannes Andenaes, one of the strongest and most reasonable proponents of the effectiveness of these laws, states the relevant caution:

What has been described is the situation as it presents itself to many middle class or upper middle class groups. How far it fits the bill for other social groups, for example professional chauffeurs or young persons, is more uncertain. It may be the case that there has been a tendency to overestimate the general deterrent effect of our strict drinking-and-driving provisions because those who usually take part in the public discussion of them make generalizations based on their own and their acquaintances' reactions. Politicians, judges, professors, policemen, and traffic safety experts, generally speaking, allow themselves to be motivated by the threat of punishment. These are groups that would experience a prison sentence for drunken driving as a social catastrophe, and they consist of people who generally have a considerable ability to control momentary impulses. In their social circles drunken driving would be regarded with astonishment, anxiety, and disapproval. Besides they can comfortably afford to hire a taxi as an alternative to driving themselves. Making a generalization from this circle to the whole body of motorists is obviously risky. Systematic studies of the conduct or attitudes within different groups of motorists are not available. [1978, pp. 38-39]

A second argument offered for the effectiveness of the Scandinavian laws cites the relative stability of the rate of recorded violations over time in the face of increasing traffic, occasional modifications of the laws in the direction of greater restraint on motorists, and greater alcohol consumption. This relative stability has been claimed as evidence of deterrence (Ross 1975, p. 294). However, the argument is not satisfactory because any number of factors could explain a constant official violation rate, especially where the known violations are a very small proportion of total estimated illegal behavior. This constancy could, for instance, be a reflection of a constant amount of resources being devoted to the control system of police and courts. As found during my visit to Scandinavia:

That diametrically opposed conclusions can be drawn from the same data used to support the deterrence hypothesis in this argument is indicated by the official opinion of the MHF [the Swedish Temperance Motorists' Association] that the doubling of *absolute* numbers of arrests from 1950 to 1967 indicates that the problem of drinking and driving is *not* under control. [Ross 1975, p. 294]

Similar evidence is raised in Andenaes's recent article—namely, that violation rates per 100,000 registered vehicles in Norway actually declined following the legislation of 1936. However, examination of the curve suggests that the decline was part of a larger secular fall in the violation rate during the 1930s, and the change in slope does not appear to be significant. Even if this were not the case, the evidence still could be met with the rejoinder that violation rates are a product of official activity and have no necessary relationship to the amount of actual drinking and driving on the highways. For instance, it might have been that the legal control system experienced some temporary difficulties in adapting to the new formulation of the offense, which would have produced the one-year dip in formal violations noted by Andenaes. Given the failure of fatalities to follow the shape of the violations curve after 1936, Andenaes's point lacks convincing power.

A third argument is based on the impression that alcohol is less often found in the blood of fatally injured drivers in Scandinavian countries than elsewhere. According to the director of MHF:

The recently presented Swedish report concerning the legislation about drunken driving calculates that of the total number of fatal casualties in road accidents in Sweden, between 10 percent and 30 percent occur in accidents involving drivers under the influence of alcohol. Even if the proportion of drivers under the influence of alcohol is disturbingly high, the fact is that it seems to be about 20 percent lower than in countries with more liberal regulations. If drunken driving in Sweden were to deteriorate so that the proportion of fatal accidents involving alcohol rose from 30 percent to the "international" level of 50 percent, it is possible to work out mathematically that the total number of fatal accidents in this country per year would increase . . . . It is reasonable to assume that thanks to our relatively stringent and consistent legislation nearly 500 lives are saved on our roads every year. [Surell n.d.]

The problem with this argument is that it is not well supported by the facts. Neither Snortum nor I have been able to find any studies of Swedish fatalities showing as few as 10 percent of drivers with illegal blood-alcohol concentrations. Rather, the literature finds illegal concentrations in 25 to 32 percent of Swedish drivers killed in crashes (SOU 1970, p. 61; Hansson 1972; Bonnichsen and Lingmark 1972; Bonnichsen and Åquist 1968) and 27 to 45 percent of Norwegian drivers killed in crashes (Lundevall and Olaisen

1976; Andenaes and Sørensen 1979). Although these figures are lower than those reported in the United States—around 50 percent is typical—they are not necessarily lower than those found in other countries (see, for example, table 4-2 for data on the United Kingdom). Furthermore, several Scandinavian studies have reported unexpectedly high proportions of injured drivers, up to 46 percent, with illegal blood-alcohol concentrations (Bø et al. 1974; see also Reigstad, Bredesen, and Lunde 1977, Ringkjøb and Lereim 1977; Bjerver, Goldberg, and Linde 1955; Linköping Hospital unpublished; Bonnichsen and Solarz 1980).

More impressive is the fact that roadside surveys of Scandinavian drivers find proportions with illegal blood-alcohol concentrations well below those reported in some other countries. In Sweden, where participation in the surveys is mandatory, two nighttime studies found no more than 2.7 percent of drivers with illegal blood-alcohol concentrations; five studies at less-restricted times found less than 1 percent. Two nighttime studies in Norway likewise found fewer than 3 percent of drivers with illegal blood-alcohol concentrations (Snortum 1981, table 2). Nighttime surveys in the United States typically find 7 or 8 percent and more of drivers with similar concentrations, although again lower levels are found in many other countries (see the sections on France and the Netherlands).

In interpreting these data it is necessary to confront the paradox of low proportions of alcohol-influenced drivers on the road yielding a relatively high proportion of killed and injured drivers with illegal blood-alcohol concentrations. If the Scandinavian approach has deterred the non-crash-involved drivers, why has it failed to prevent the crash-involved from drinking? One possible response is offered by Andenaes, who noted that the crash-involved drinking drivers frequently are people with alcohol problems and other social-adjustment difficulties:

> The groups in question here present poor targets for the law's deterrent and moral effect. In short, it is reasonable to believe that the law's motivating effect is strongest among those who would have represented only a moderate traffic accident risk even if they had consumed alcohol in excess of the legal limit. [1978, p. 46]

Another serious problem in interpreting this evidence is that, while it may be compatible with a deterrence explanation, it is also compatible with the idea that other differences between the Scandinavian countries and comparison jurisdictions affect the level of alcohol consumed by drivers. Examples of these factors—evident to anyone who stays more than a few days in the Scandinavian countries—are different patterns of alcohol use, including abstention at most times (Nordegren 1981), legal controls over the availability of alcoholic beverages, and different patterns of vehicle ownership and use.

The frequency of personal and social pathology among those convicted of drinking and driving is sometimes cited as a fourth argument for the deterrent effectiveness of the Scandinavian laws, the inference being that people without serious drinking problems have been deterred from drinking and driving. Observers point to the prevalence of very young drivers and older blue-collar alcoholics in the population imprisoned for drinking-and-driving offenses. However, the conclusion does not follow. Mentally healthy white-collar Scandinavians may refrain from drinking and driving for a variety of reasons, among which the legal restriction is only one. Furthermore, the finding of personal and social pathology among drinking drivers occurs in jurisdictions where it is impossible to claim any deterrent value on behalf of the drinking-and-driving laws (Ross 1975, p. 298).

A fifth argument offered for the deterrent effectiveness of the Scandinavian laws concerns the public knowledge of, and support for, these laws found in survey data. The data need not be challenged, although implications that support is greater in Scandinavia than elsewhere are not necessarily correct (Ross 1975, p. 296). Hauge has recently demonstrated that the details of the Norwegian law are widely known and that the 50-milligram level "has become part of the moral climate" (1978, p. 68). Knowledge of a law is a prerequisite to its deterrent effectiveness, and we may concede that this prerequisite has been fulfilled. However, it is a necessary but not sufficient condition for deterrence, and the argument goes no further.

The claim of a scientific demonstration of deterrence for the Scandinavian model has recently been put forward by Harold Votey in papers applying correlational analysis to data on naturally occurring variation over time in Norway and among counties in Sweden. Votey's claims are strongly worded:

> This analysis and the accompanying empirical evidence indicate that apparent ambiguities in the data which measure drinking, driving and law enforcement activities can be sorted out with the use of models that specifically account for the interrelationships that jointly generate the data. Furthermore, it appears that fundamental theories of deterrence are supported by the data, once the simultaneity of the relationships is specified. [1978, p. 96]

To this reader, the argument and methodology of Votey's work are so poorly communicated as to be nearly incomprehensible. The method of correlational analysis is known to suffer from very serious flaws, as stated in the National Academy of Sciences' review of the literature (Blumstein, Cohen, and Nagin 1978). Some scholars have arrived at the conclusion that these problems are so fundamental as to render the method virtually useless for the study of deterrence (Cook 1979).

Concerning Votey's specific application of the method, the best advice available to me (Zador 1978) suggests that an arbitrary selection of input variables and a variety of debatable assumptions concerning their formal status negate the elegance of the mathematical models and statistical procedures used to process them. Because of the large number of variables used and short length of the data series, it is not difficult to find close fits between expected and empirical values in this type of exercise. The proof of the pudding will be in Votey's ability to predict future values from his econometric model. In the interim, it would seem that little reliance should be placed on the results of his analysis.

Votey's studies also fail to address the question of whether the Scandinavian laws provide greater deterrence than classical drinking-and-driving laws that are comparably enforced. His studies claim to find that, in Sweden and Norway, over time or across jurisdictions, greater inputs of law enforcement result in fewer crashes. However, his time-series data do not cover any period during which classical laws were in effect, and his cross-sectional studies likewise are irrelevant to what law enforcement might accomplish under a classical law. Votey's work may be relevant to the question of the effects of law enforcement but it is irrelevant to the effects of the particular features of Norwegian and Swedish legislation.

My position on the evidence for deterrence by the Norwegian and Swedish laws frequently has been misunderstood because I titled my original report (1975) "The Scandinavian Myth." What is mythical about the Scandinavian experience is the idea that scientifically acceptable evidence exists to demonstrate the simple deterrent effectiveness of the laws of 1936 and 1941. The present review of the evidence should make it clear that I did not claim to have disproved the general preventive effectiveness of the Scandinavian approach to drinking-and-driving law. My choice of title was made in part as a warning signal to policymakers and those inclined to support the wholesale transportation of the Scandinavian model to other jurisdictions in the expectation of a proven deterrent solution to the worldwide problem of drinking and driving.

I do not believe that the available evidence supports the idea that the Scandinavian countries achieved important increments in simple deterrence with adoptions of their laws in 1936 and 1941. However, it now seems to me unreasonable to have expected much in the way of increments in deterrence from these laws, given their history and the specifications of deterrence theory. Moreover, the state of the data and the presence of important perturbations of the social scene in the 1930s and 1940s make it difficult to apply not only interrupted time-series analysis but also virtually all scientific methods to the study of the immediate effects of these laws.

There does exist a set of facts compatible with the idea that the Scandinavian countries have achieved some general prevention in the matter of drinking and driving from the application of their approach over the long run, perhaps through the mechanisms of habit formation and moral education (Andenaes 1974). This evidence has been summarized in the last few pages. Matters such as the very low proportion of alcohol-influenced drivers on the highways, the great knowledge of and support for the laws, and so on are compatible with this notion, and the case is well made by Snortum. That the case is not straightforward is indicated by the paradoxically high blood-alcohol concentrations in the bodies of people killed and injured and the existence of important rival explanations due to differences between Scandinavian and comparison societies in matters relating to alcohol, driving, and law. Moreover, the actual risk of apprehension for drinking drivers in Scandinavia appears to be relatively low (Persson 1978), and drivers appear to perceive this fact (SOU 1970). In other countries, this situation seems to have resulted in demonstrable declines in the simple deterrent effects of Scandinavian-type laws over a relatively short period of time.

In sum, I am persuaded by Andenaes and Snortum that a plausible case can be made for the long-run effectiveness of the Scandinavian laws in Scandinavia, although the case is complex and far from proven. Moreover, the punitive details of the existing laws have not been shown to be necessary. Klette (1978) characterizes the Scandinavian leadership as being uninterested in further inquiry into these matters; they have little to gain and much to lose (for example, governmental subsidies of temperance organizations) through more-detailed knowledge. It seems to me that, although little can be learned at this point from further historical studies of the Scandinavian laws, much of theoretical and practical value could be learned from modest innovations—namely, varying actual certainty, severity, and celerity of punishment and looking for further deterrent effects (which are surely needed, despite the apparent official complacency). I would also argue (Ross 1978, p. 59) that imprisonment of thousands of people for many weeks on the basis of a scientifically unfounded belief in the necessity of such punishment should be considered dubious social policy and that controlled social experimentation would be possible with regard to this question. That the politics of the northern countries preclude such experimentation strikes me as most unfortunate.

Conclusion

This chapter has reviewed the literature on evaluations of the adoption of Scandinavian-type laws in a variety of countries. Despite the wide range of specific laws and evaluation techniques, there seems to be a convergence of findings. In general, adoption of Scandinavian-type laws produces evidence of a deterrent effect on indicators of drinking and driving, including crash-related deaths and injuries. The effect seems to be greater in those instances in which the innovation is more controversial, more publicized, and more newsworthy. Since the fundamental variables in the deterrence model are perceptual, this finding is theoretically expected, although officials battling what they deem to be an unreasonable opposition often have not seen the benefits of that opposition for achieving their deterrence goals.

Conversely, wherever evidence of deterrence has been noted, it has proved to be evanescent. Simple deterrence, the modification of behavior through fear of legal punishment, has not endured in the experiences reviewed. I speculate that the initial deterrent results and their subsequent decay are due to an initial overestimation of the probability of punishment, produced by the publicity and newsworthiness of the new laws, followed by drivers learning through experience that the risk of punishment remains negligible.

The experiences of Norway and Sweden suggest the possibility that drinking and driving can be affected by law through mechanisms related to, but broader than, simple deterrence—those labeled habit formation and moral education by Andenaes. These mechanisms are understood to depend on maintenance of a simple deterrence-based legal prohibition over time. A plausible case can be made for the Scandinavians' having achieved such results from their long efforts to control drinking and driving through law. However, the case is not proved, and many questions can be raised about it. Perhaps the most fundamental is whether and how the Norwegians and Swedes were able to maintain the perception of threat so as to produce long-range effects when the likelihood of punishment for violators seems to have been as negligible in Scandinavia as anywhere else.

5 Law Enforcement

The component of deterrence that is termed *certainty,* or *likelihood,* of punishment may be subject to deliberate increase in police enforcement campaigns. This is especially likely where police activity is proactive (that is, not dependent on a victim to demand attention), as in the case of drinking and driving. Of course, to be directly relevant to the deterrence model, increased police activity must be known or perceived by the relevant public. Perhaps enforcement campaigns of very large magnitude can become self-evident to drivers through experience, but most such campaigns in practice employ publicity to affect public perception more directly and immediately.

On the whole, the experiences reported in this chapter are supportive of deterrence. Although the examples are not as numerous as one might like, and although the evaluation methods are frequently deficient, in the case of law-enforcement campaigns as in adoptions of Scandinavian-type laws, there is a convergence of findings favorable to deterrence theory.

The Cheshire Blitz

By 1975, the Road Safety Act of 1967 was considered a failure by many experts in the United Kingdom. Indicators such as the ratio of nighttime to daytime crashes and the proportions of illegal blood-alcohol concentrations among drivers killed in crashes returned to, and even surpassed, levels prevailing in 1966. The provisions of the Road Safety Act were embodied with little change in the Road Traffic Act of 1972, but the original legislation had fallen so low in official regard that a Royal Commission was established to examine the situation. In this context, a police chief in a provincial county performed a social experiment that, although unnoticed by national authorities, demonstrated convincingly the potential for deterrence of the existing legislation when accompanied by an enforcement campaign.

Word of this experiment reached me as rumor during a visit to England in the spring of 1976. Officials at the Transport and Road Research Laboratory and in the Ministry of Transport and the Home Office knew nothing of it, but the source was tracked down by Dr. John Havard at the British Medical Association, who put me in touch with Chief Constable William Kelsall of Cheshire. A brief visit to this county obtained the local statistics and other materials for my report, "Deterrence Regained" (Ross 1977), which I now summarize.

Although U.K. police, unlike police in the United States, are nationally coordinated, considerable discretion rests in the various constabularies in the manner of enforcing the law. Concerned about the apparent falling off of the drinking-and-driving law's effectiveness, the chief of the Midlands county of Cheshire in 1975 decided to conduct an "experiment . . . to go as far as we could within the law to breathalise all people driving between ten at night and two in the morning." He required that policemen under his authority administer the screening breath tests in the course of all investigations of crashes and of traffic-law violations during these nighttime hours for one week during July. There resulted 284 breath tests during the "experimental" period, compared with 31 in the same period of the previous year. Subsequently, 38 drivers were found to have had illegal blood-alcohol concentrations, compared with 13 in the prior year. Although testing in the normal year was proportionately more likely to find positive results, it appeared that numbers of alcohol-influenced drivers had been escaping detection even though involved in law violations or crashes and therefore susceptible to the requirement of breath tests.

Chief Kelsall then expanded the "experimental" period to include the hours of 9 P.M. to 4 A.M., obtained a control sample from the hours of 2 P.M. to 5 P.M., and maintained the campaign for virtually the entire month of September 1975. However, as word of the experiment spread, the chief became the object of vehement protest by representatives of automobile clubs and local political figures who claimed that the effort was equivalent to random testing, which Parliament had specifically eliminated from the Road Safety Act. Kelsall refused to yield to this pressure as a matter of principle. His support was sufficient to enable him to complete the month's effort, which then took on the characteristics of a visible and even notorious enforcement campaign.

As with the Road Safety Act at its inception, the Cheshire blitz was associated with a diminution in serious crashes that was officially interpreted as an effect of the campaign. Interrupted time-series analysis of fatal and serious-injury crashes supports this interpretation, even though the analysis is less powerful in dealing with the smaller data base and less-detailed statistics were available for Cheshire than for the country as a whole.

The data for all serious crashes are presented in figure 5-1. The drop in September 1975 is statistically significant (and, incidentally, no drop occurred in July when the increased enforcement was not publicized). The inference of a deterrent effect for the September campaign is reinforced by the evidence in figure 5-2 concerning serious crashes during drinking hours. The decline in this figure does not quite reach statistical significance because of the great variability in the number of crashes in this small data base, but it can be viewed as strongly suggestive, especially as the curve for low-

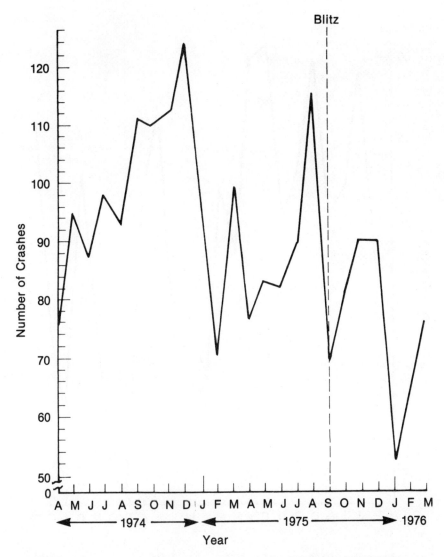

Figure 5-1. Crashes Producing Serious or Fatal Injuries in Cheshire, England

alcohol-consumption hours (not shown) shows no such change associated with the blitz.

During the course of the Cheshire breathaliser blitz, the level of breath testing in the county rose to six times the national average. Whether such a

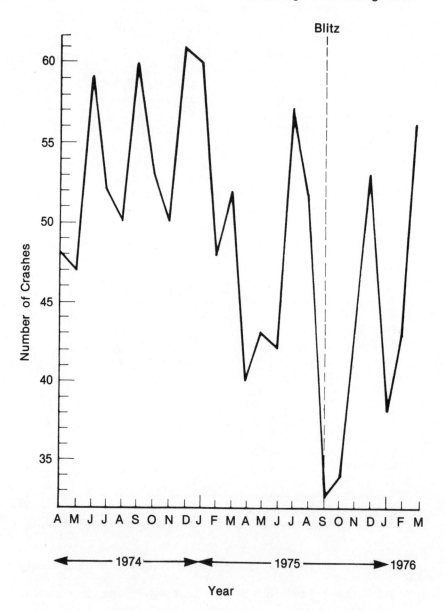

Source: Ross 1977, p. 247. Copyright by The University of Chicago Press. Reprinted with permission.

Figure 5-2. Total Crashes during Drinking Hours (10 P.M. to 4 A.M.) in Cheshire, England

level is necessary to obtain the achieved results, whether it would be sufficient to maintain an effect over the longer run, and how the actual enforcement interacted with its newsworthiness to produce a decline in drinking and driving are among the important but unanswered questions relevant to this experience.

In sum, although the nationwide deterrent effect of the British Road Safety Act of 1967 appears largely to have dissipated within a few years, this effect was regained in the course of a limited local increment of enforcement and (inadvertent) publicity.

The New Zealand Blitzes

It may be recalled from chapter 4 that the evaluator of New Zealand's adoption of a Scandinavian-type drinking-and-driving law, Paul Hurst, concluded that little, if any, deterrence was accomplished by this law. (On the basis of the data he presented, I saw somewhat more evidence than he did consistent with deterrence predictions, but it is not a strong case.) Later, in his post at the New Zealand Ministry of Transport, Hurst obtained the report of the Cheshire blitz and interested his colleagues in mounting similar campaigns in New Zealand. He entitled his report of the results "Deterrence at Last" (Hurst and Wright 1980).

The New Zealand campaigns involved enforcement of the 1969 drinking-and-driving law, modified by amendments in 1971 and 1974. These campaigns are described as follows:

> The nationwide blitz began at noon of 15 July (a Saturday) and continued through Monday 31 July. It was heralded by a week's advance publicity taking the form of media announcements. These were followed by paid advertisements in radio, television and newspapers which began on 17 July and continued until 5 August, five days after the end of the enforcement campaign.
>
> The motorist, who had been told when the campaign would begin, also knew what tactics *might* be employed. . . . He had reasons to believe that, if he were stopped by an enforcement officer, there was an increased chance of being breath tested (on suspicion of having recently been drinking). He also knew that there was an increased chance that he would be stopped by an enforcement officer, especially during the popular drinking hours. [Hurst and Wright 1980]

Concerning the second campaign:

> A publicity campaign commenced on 4 December 1978 with advertisements in newspapers, and on radio. It was aimed to reach the late teen-early twenty group. A traffic officer was featured in a half page newspaper advertisement presenting a rather threatening message and image. . . .

One additional factor that reinforced specific blitz publicity was that the New Zealand legislature, on 1 December 1978, passed new legal provisions aimed at the drinking driver. The main provisions were a raising of the monetary maximum for conviction from $400 to $1500, the lowering of the blood alcohol limit to 80 milligrams/100 millilitres and the introduction of an absolute breath alcohol limit of 500 micrograms per litre. At the same time, evidential breath testing was introduced, although the availability of testing devices was limited. [Hurst and Wright 1970]

Both blitzes involved increased police activity. The number of screening tests was quadrupled in the first effort and doubled in the second. Moreover, in the second campaign, publicity generated public consternation, and the automobile association complained that random alcohol checks were being made under the pretext of vehicle-equipment checks—situations reminiscent of Cheshire and likely to have enhanced the effect of the paid publicity through media attention.

Evaluation of the New Zealand blitzes seems to have been more effectively guided by methodological principles than the evaluation of the 1969 law. There was also greater success in obtaining appropriate data series. Unlike the prior evaluation, this one "did not consider the officially reported rate of alcohol involvement, considering this to be worse than useless at a time of dramatically increased concern over the drinking driver" (Hurst and Wright 1980). Instead, the evaluation employed a variety of interesting and innovative indicators of drinking and driving, including, for example, observations of liquor consumption in two rental ballrooms in Auckland for eleven evenings prior to the first blitz, nine during the blitz, and seventeen afterwards. Average milliliters of absolute alcohol consumed were 75.8, 67.8, and 82.7 respectively. In the absence of prior years' data to indicate seasonal variations, the analysts did not test these differences for significance but merely regarded them as suggestive of a deterrent effect.

Another measure used to evaluate the New Zealand campaigns was car-park occupancy at selected hotels and taverns in Auckland and Christchurch late on Friday evenings. The results, shown in figure 5-3, again are reasonably in accord with predictions from the deterrence model.

A drop also appeared in road injuries reported by twenty cooperating hospitals during the first blitz (see figure 5-4). The second blitz was evaluated with similiar data furnished by an initial twenty-three cooperating hospitals, joined later by three others in Auckland; both data series are illustrated in figure 5-5. These time-series graphs are essentially in harmony with expectations, although the interpretations would be more securely-based had the series been somewhat more extensive.

Claims filed with the Accident Compensation Commission were analyzed depending on whether they occurred during "main drinking hours" or at other times of the week. The ratio is graphed, with the previous year for

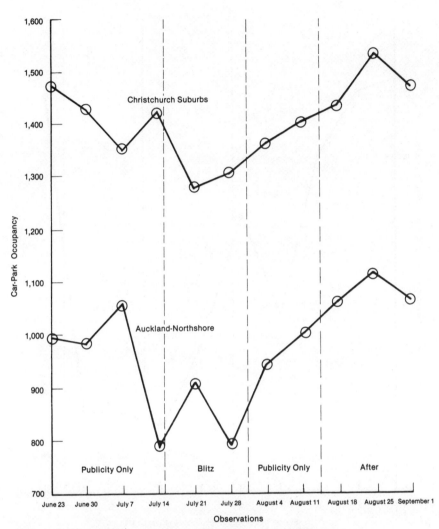

Source: Hurst and Wright 1980, figure 1. Reprinted with permission.

Figure 5-3. Car-Park Occupancy for Selected Taverns in Christchurch and Auckland, New Zealand, in the Vicinity of an Enforcement Blitz

comparison, in figure 5-6 for the first blitz and figure 5-7 for the second. Due to the presence of prior trends it would be easier to interpret these curves, especially figure 5-7, if the time series were more extended and if the comparison curve were composed of data from more than one year. However, the results again are supportive of deterrence, and the cumulation

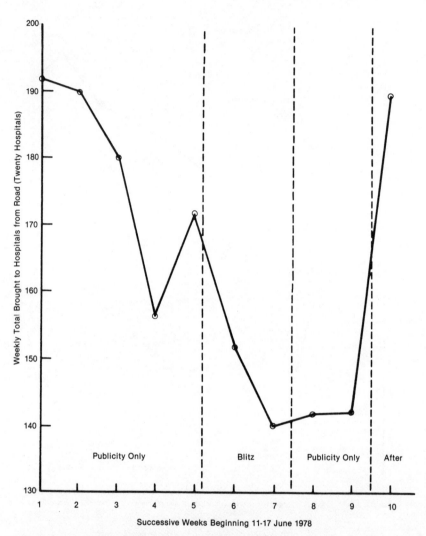

Source: Hurst and Wright 1980, figure 2. Reprinted with permission.

Figure 5-4. Crash-Involved Drivers Hospitalized in Selected Hospitals in New Zealand in the Vicinity of an Enforcement Blitz

of a variety of fallible data compensates for the weaknesses in any particular demonstration.

Total serious crashes were analyzed in a variety of ways, one of which is presented in figure 5-8, which shows the ratio of nighttime to daytime crashes and which seems particularly convincing. Fatalities, graphed in

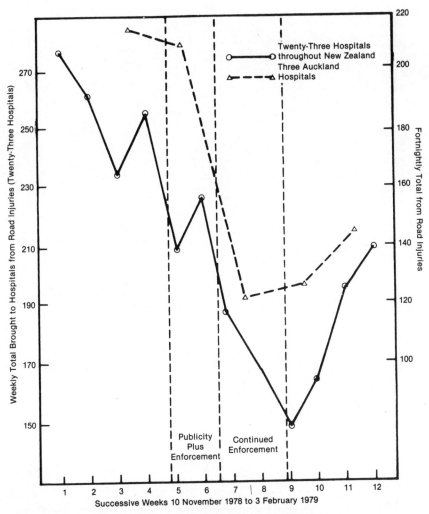

Source: Hurst and Wright 1980, figure 3. Reprinted with permission.

Figure 5-5. Crash-Involved Drivers Hospitalized in Selected Hospitals in New Zealand in the Vicinity of the Second Blitz

figure 5-9, did not furnish much evidence for the effect of the first blitz, although the second one does seem to be reflected in the curves. The only indicator studied that failed to reflect an appropriate change for either blitz was the ratio of single-vehicle to multiple-vehicle crashes.

In light of the numerous analyses, and despite the negative results for single-vehicle crashes, I would not want to quarrel with Hurst and Wright's

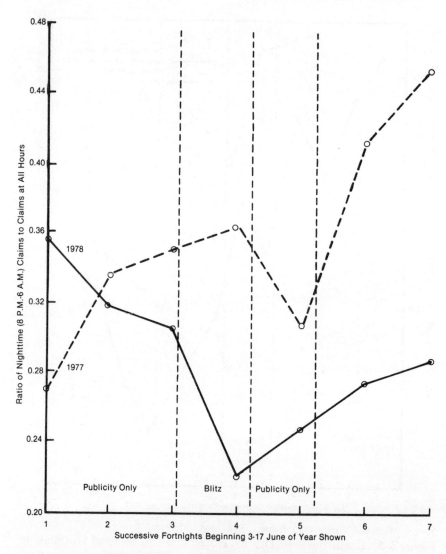

Source: Hurst and Wright 1980, figure 5. Reprinted with permission.

Figure 5-6. Ratio of Nighttime to Total Accident Compensation Claims in New Zealand in the Vicinity of an Enforcement Blitz

(1980) conclusion that "each of the two enforcement blitzes reduced the road losses that normally accrue from alcohol impaired driving." One might note the limited nature of these blitzes; as in Cheshire, they had definite terminations, and all indexes show that either immediately or after

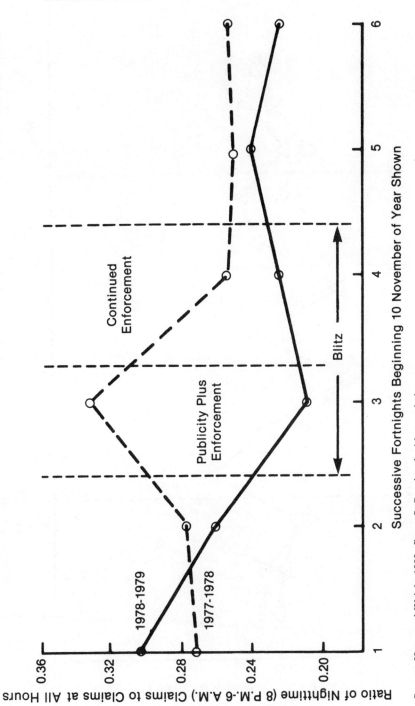

Source: Hurst and Wright 1980, figure 7. Reprinted with permission.

Figure 5-7. Ratio of Nighttime to Total Accident Compensation Claims in New Zealand in the Vicinity of the Second Blitz

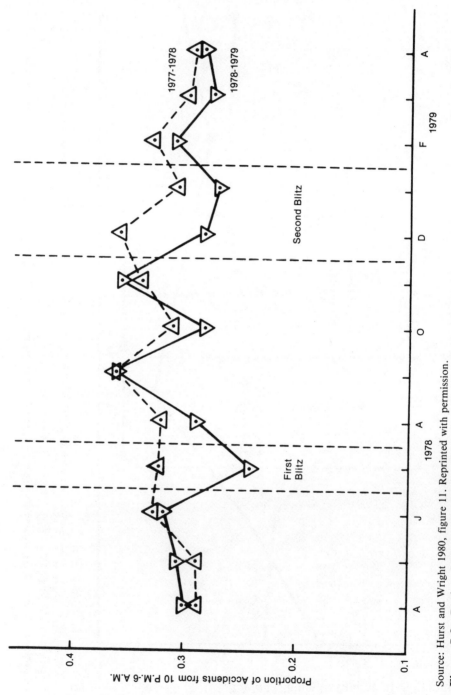

Source: Hurst and Wright 1980, figure 11. Reprinted with permission.

Figure 5-8. Ratio of Nighttime to Total Serious Crashes in New Zealand in the Vicinity of the Enforcement Blitzes

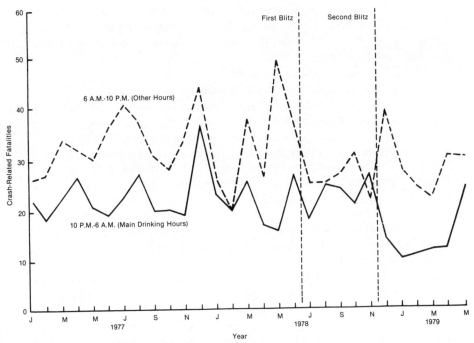

Source: Hurst and Wright 1980, figure 9. Reprinted with permission.
Note: Figures after June 1978 are subject to adjustment.
Figure 5-9. Crash-Related Fatalities in New Zealand in the Vicinity of the
Enforcement Blitzes

a short lag things looked very much as before. No permanent change seems
to have been achieved.

"Random" Breath Testing in Victoria

The Australian state of Victoria maintained its early-bird status by adopting
provisions for "random"—actually, arbitrary—breath testing of drivers in
1976. This was the same year that such a practice was first permanently
legitimized in Scandinavia and fully two years prior to its adoption in
France. Testing of drivers without the need for police to suspect alcoholic
influence was permitted in predetermined roadblocks. The law was little-
used at its inception; "random" patrol hours in Melbourne averaged about
eight hours per week, and roadblocks apparently were not used in the coun-
tryside at all. However, in 1977, two periods of intensified enforcement occurred in Melbourne when patrol hours were quadrupled; late in 1978, a

further enforcement campaign increased the number of roadblock-patrol hours to 100 per week. These operations were concentrated in four distinct sectors of the city to increase their local impact and to strengthen the possiblilty of evaluation.

The 1977 campaigns were evaluated in an unreported pilot project that yielded "highly suggestive" but not conclusive demonstrations of effectiveness, leading to a more-elaborate evaluation reported in a conference paper (Cameron, Strang, and Vulcan 1980). The methodology of this study has been extensively criticized, and more-recent unreported work has been undertaken to strengthen it. Criterion variables included crash fatalities, serious casualty crashes, and blood-alcohol concentrations among nighttime-driver casualties. The perceived risk of detection for drinking and driving also was measured by survey techniques. The authors reached their conclusions by comparing the level of a criterion variable (for example, nighttime fatalities) in the patrolled area with the level of the same variable in the same area in the prior year, corrected for changes during an earlier control nonpatrolled period in the same two years. A net reduction was computed by deducting the second change from the first. The statistical significance of the change seems to have been measured by simple chi-square tests. Although this procedure is perhaps somewhat better than a mere before-and-after comparison, since it at least partially controls for maturation and instability, it is uncontrolled for history that, with only one comparison year, is a very plausible rival hypothesis. The statistical test also is not the best one available for this type of data so that doubts are raised about the control for instability.

Putting aside technical questions, the findings of the study support deterrence-based expectations. There were significant decreases during the 1978 enforcement campaign in nighttime fatal crashes and serious-casualty crashes, as well as in driver casualties with illegal blood-alcohol concentrations (the latter in single-vehicle crashes only). The perception of probable apprehension for driving while drinking increased during the 1977 campaigns over the prelaw period, and it increased even more during the 1978 campaign when the question described the drinking as "not obvious." Perception of the likelihood of apprehension for drinking and driving increased more than perception of the likelihood of apprehension for speeding, which was used as a control.

As with the other enforcement campaigns reported here, the Victorian study did not attempt to measure persistence of the observed changes beyond the termination of the campaigns; apparently the changes were not expected to survive these campaigns.

The reported evaluation of the Victorian campaigns, although not as methodologically strong as one might like, yields conclusions that resemble those reached in most other studies of short-term-enforcement efforts. Going beyond the other reported studies, the Victorian report yields evidence of a predicted change in perceptions of risk of apprehension, which is consistent with the deterrence model.

Canada's R.I.D.E.

Staff members of the Addiction Research Foundation of Ontario have reported some results of an enforcement campaign based on the 1969 Canadian law. Impact was found in survey results, including increased perceived risk of being apprehended when drinking and driving. However, no significant changes were found in behavior indexed by crashes. The study is of interest primarily for its description of how to achieve "random" enforcement under a law that requires reasonable cause to suspect the influence of alcohol before permitting a breath test.

R.I.D.E. was a program concerned with "reducing impaired driving in Etobicoke," a part of Toronto. Police established roadblocks at over 100 locations chosen for visibility, the occurrence of crashes, and the estimated likelihood of yielding drinking drivers. In the first twelve months of the campaign, which was planned to last eighteen months, 132,000 cars were stopped:

> The officers randomly stopped motorists [under the authority of the Ontario Highway Traffic Act which allows an officer to determine whether the driver is in possession of a valid license], and they identified themselves as part of the R.I.D.E. program, explained its objectives, and asked for the driver's license. . . . During this process, the R.I.D.E. officer watched the driver for signs of drinking. [Vingilis and Salutin 1980, p. 269]

If alcohol was suspected—for example, by odor of drink on the breath, a glimpse of an opened beverage bottle, or admission by the driver that he had been drinking or was coming from a drinking establishment—the policeman requested a breath test that, if positive, led to further steps toward prosecution. Slightly more than 1 percent of drivers were requested to take the test, suggesting (given the sites selected) that only a small fraction of drinking drivers was apprehended by this program. However, deterrence and not prosecution was the program's principal aim.

R.I.D.E. was publicized by a pamphlet mailed to every household in the district, but surveys revealed that the main source of knowledge of the program was either the media or personal experience at a roadblock.

The survey was accomplished in three waves, one before and two during the campaign, and control samples from elsewhere in Toronto were gathered for each phase. The report notes that residents of Etobicoke exhibited increased knowledge about drinking and driving and that their estimates of "the average man's risk" (but not "my risk") of apprehension for drinking and driving increased.

Estimates of actual drinking and driving in the district were based-largely on inappropriate data (police estimates and charges filed). Although these showed no clear evidence of deterrence, the results are probably irrelevant. The one potentially valid measure—blood-alcohol concentrations among drivers involved in crashes—did not vary as expected.

The negative findings in this instance perhaps can be explained by the difficulties involved in reliance on data from a small jurisdiction embedded in a larger community (drivers crashing in Etobicoke may reside elsewhere in Toronto). However, the demonstration that perceived risk of apprehension may be increased as a result of an enforcement campaign is a welcome footnote to the other literature on law enforcement in this area.

The U.S. ASAPs

Some American readers may be surprised to learn that U.S. laws with respect to drinking and driving largely conform to the Scandinavian model. The Uniform Vehicle Code, which serves as a model for state laws, prohibits driving with a blood-alcohol concentration of 0.10 percent. Equalling or exceeding this limit is a per se violation (Section 11-902a) (the tolerated level is close to the one contained in the British Road Safety Act, which proscribes driving with more than 0.08 percent blood-alcohol concentration). Chemical testing for blood alcohol is mandated (Section 11-902.1). Refusal to provide appropriate samples can be used as evidence in a drinking-and-driving prosecution (Section 11-902.2) and automatically results in license suspension (Section 6-205). The code provides for mandatory prison on a first conviction of drinking and driving (Section 11-902.2), although exceptions are provided to permit diversion to treatment.

The main gap between the Uniform Vehicle Code and the strict Scandinavian model for drinking-and-driving laws is the lack of provision in the code for testing blood-alcohol concentrations prior to arrest (that is, prior to a police officer's independent suspicion of alcohol influence). This gap may rule out roadblocks on the Australian or French model but would permit practices like those in Norway or Canada.

A current review of drinking-and-driving laws in the various states finds that aspects of the Scandinavian model appear in the formal laws of all U.S. jurisdictions (U.S. Department of Transportation 1979a). A blood-alcohol concentration is specified in the laws of all states, usually leading to a presumption of impairment but establishing a per se violation in at least thirteen states. The limit is 0.10 percent everywhere except Utah and Idaho, where it is 0.08 percent. The requirement for a driver to submit to chemical testing for blood alcohol is universal, with the penalty for refusing usually being loss of driver's license under the doctrine of implied consent. In twelve states, prison is provided as a sanction for a first offense of drinking and driving, and additional states prescribe it on second and subsequent offenses. License suspension for violators is mandatory almost everywhere, although usually only for second and subsequent offenses. Formal law in the United States thus largely embodies the Scandinavian approach to drinking and driving. However, practitioners and observers have found that informal law, or law in action, is very different (Gusfield 1981).

One of the first activities of the newly formed Department of Transportation was a study of the relationship between alcohol and highway safety. The report of this study (U.S. Department of Transportation 1968) made politically visible the fact that even moderate drinking and driving is associated with strongly increased crash risk and that heavy drinkers apparently play a major role in the problem. Alcohol Safety Action Projects (ASAPs) were launched by the Department of Transportation during the 1970s in response to this definition of the drinking-and-driving problem.

ASAPs were not conceived as embodying radical changes. Each of the thirty-five programs utilized principally existing community agencies—police, courts, schools, and so forth,—coordinated in a systems approach and fortified with additional resources ($78 million in federal funds, plus matching state and local contributions). ASAPs centered on the task of using the legal system to identify "problem drinkers" and to refer them to appropriate treatment facilities.

From the viewpoint of the deterrence model, the principal changes associated with the ASAPs were increases in police patrol and improvements in the efficiency of processing drinking drivers in the courts. In other words, changes were in the direction of increased certainty of apprehension and conviction, along with increased celerity of conviction. No effort was made to increase penalties for drinking and driving. Rather, the penalties were de facto reduced due to the provision for diversion of large numbers of offenders from routine punishment to treatment.

With few exceptions, the ASAPs were successful in providing major increases in the actual probability of apprehension of drinking drivers. This was achieved partly by the use of special ASAP-financed police patrols and partly by increases in the sensitization of regular patrols to drinking drivers. Arrests for drinking and driving increased many times over; the typical ASAP increased arrests by a factor of 2.5, and in one case the increase was by a factor of 44 (U.S. Department of Transportation 1979b). Of course, some proportion of those arrested could have been drivers who previously would have been apprehended but charged with a violation other than drinking and driving, perhaps one easier to prosecute. However, even a shift in the legal label from a less-serious to a more-serious offense might be expected to have some positive deterrent results, and there is no question that many of the drinking drivers apprehended during the ASAPs would not have been noticed under conditions of patrol prevailing before the projects.

The ASAP experience provides an opportunity to study the short-run deterrent effect of increased law enforcement on drinking and driving because the other intended goals of the project, including treatment and education of apprehended violators, would most likely be achieved, if at all, only in the long run. Moreover, drivers experiencing ASAP-sponsored treatment programs would be relatively few in the total population of drinking drivers; therefore, important changes in the general statistics could not reasonably be attributed to the achievement of goals other than increased law enforcement.

Evaluations were presented by the individual ASAPs, but the resulting documents are not as enlightening as was hoped. One source of interpretive difficulty is the heterogeneity of ASAP programs and sites. The projects were united in their general approach to controlling drinking and driving, but their specifics were highly diverse. The differences were unsystematic and unhelpful as controls for analytical purposes. For political reasons, among others, the sites were chosen in a manner that for evaluation purposes must be described as haphazard. The quality of implementation varied enormously.

Also, the quality of individual ASAP evaluations generally was poor. Of thirty project reports submitted to the Department of Transportation in 1973, only six were judged to be based on strong analyses. In the following year, only nine of twenty-one reports merited this judgment. (In general, the better studies were less supportive of pro-ASAP changes). According to the Department of Transportation's final evaluation (1979b, p. 9), the common problems in the evaluations were inconsistent reporting of crash series, inadequate or improper testing for statistical significance, failure to consider competing explanatory hypotheses in the analyses, and conflicting ultimate performance measures at a given site.

The inadequacy of site-by-site evaluations led the Department of Transportation to design after-the-fact evaluations of the projects as a whole. Although the initial attempts at overall evaluation were methodologically flawed (Zador 1976, 1977; Johnson, Levy, and Voas 1976) the final evaluation is informative. It inquires merely into whether changes in indexes of drinking and driving occurred during ASAP operational periods. It is unconcerned with post-operational influences, and no attention seems to have been paid to the possibility of initial changes followed by reversion to the status quo during the period of operation. Properly abjuring reliance on police-reported alcohol-influence data (although this criterion frequently was used in the individual project reports), the focus of the overall evaluation is nighttime crashes, which are compared in a multiple time-series design with daytime crashes in the same communities, with experiences in matched control communities and with a national trend. The control series are crucial because the ASAPs had the misfortune to span the 1973 fuel crisis, which had a much greater influence on the crash picture than anything reasonably to be expected from interventions like the ASAPs.

With corrections for the effects of seasonality, the fuel crisis, and the 55-mph speed limit, data from twelve of the thirty-five individual projects showed statistically significant declines in nighttime crashes. Although this fraction seems relatively unimpressive, the evaluators credibly argue that sites with very low initial crash rates faced considerable difficulty in achieving large reductions (these sites probably should not have been selected for ASAPs in the first place). In addition, sites with growing populations tended to show less ASAP effect. Although the reason for this is not spelled out in the report, it could be due to associated increases in traffic, yielding increments of crashes that would have occurred in the absence of any intervention. Of the thirteen sites with three or more nighttime fatal crashes per month and a growth rate of less than 10 percent, eight showed significant reductions in nighttime fatal crashes, a more-impressive fraction. Also, a correlation between the level of enforcement and the reduction in nighttime fatalities was visible only in the thirteen high-crash, low-growth sites.

Surveys of blood-alcohol concentrations among non-crash-involved drivers in selected hours were conducted prior to the ASAPs, or early in the initiation of the programs, and again during full operation at twenty-seven sites. A significant difference occurred in the proportion of illegal blood-alcohol concentrations, dropping from 53 to 46 per thousand drivers, during operational periods.

The final evaluation of the ASAPs was a salvage operation on what, with more initial time and thought, might have been a much more-informative experiment in deterring drinking and driving. In my opinion, although the post hoc selection of control communities weakens the quasi-experimental design of the final evaluation, the analysis was well done under the circumstances. It supplied evidence supporting the proposition that some programs involving enforcement of prevailing U.S. laws could, in the short run, produce declines in drinking and driving and in associated casualties. The analysis is too approximate, and the negative cases too prominent, to conclude much beyond this.

Conclusion

This chapter is shorter, and includes fewer examples, than I had hoped given the common occurrence of enforcement campaigns designed to deter drinking and driving. The literature is sparse because many campaigns have been undertaken without competent evaluation, and more important, the results of evaluated campaigns have not been systematically published.

However, the results here converge and lead to the conclusion that enforcement campaigns can produce deterrent effects by increasing public perception of the likelihood of punishment. It should be noted that all the examples are limited in time and are not analyzed in a way that would permit determining whether their effects diminish as the campaigns continue. None of the evaluators seems to have worked with the expectation that postcampaign drinking and driving would be reduced as a result of the experience of the campaign, and the available data would not support such an expectation.

The findings of this chapter clearly relate to those of chapter 4 on adoptions of Scandinavian-type laws. Both enforcement campaigns and novel drinking-and-driving laws may increase public perception of the certainty of punishment for violators (the Scandinavian-type laws also may increase perceptions of severity of punishment; the question of severity will be investigated in chapter 6). Both the laws and enforcement campaigns are found to be effective but only in the short run. The effects of the laws are found to diminish over time, and the enforcement campaigns have been terminated with no evidence of posttermination effects.

6 Severity

The second independent variable in the theoretical model of deterrence is perceived severity of punishment. We theoretically expect that potential violators perceiving more severe penalties will refrain more from law-violating behavior. Only a few reported studies are relevant to this hypothesis; these have involved increasing the threatened severity of punishment for drinking and driving in the absence of simultaneous changes in certainty and celerity. This chapter reports on a statutory change, the Finnish law of 1950, which greatly increased the formal penalty for drinking and driving. In addition, two cases of "severity crackdowns"—a judge promising harsher sentences for drinking drivers convicted in his court—are reported.

The consequences of crashes involving alcohol concern policymakers on many levels in many countries, including the judiciary that has more or less direct control over the punishments meted out in the courts. Any judge who has discretion in sentencing can launch his own severity crackdown. As in the case of police enforcement crackdowns, there are doubtless numerous examples every year of judicial severity crackdowns; these would be worth reviewing, but they are not reported in accessible literature. Judges rarely have the opportunity to obtain competent evaluations (indeed, they may not realize this need), and there are no established modes of communication for bringing these cases to the attention of other concerned policymakers and analysts.

Although I expect the well-meaning individuals responsible for the innovations discussed here to be disappointed by my critique, their cases have not been chosen in order to expose poor management. Rather, I believe these cases were relatively well executed compared with the bulk of such crackdowns. The problem lies in the concept and not its execution.

The Finnish Law of 1950

Until very recently, the Finnish approach to controlling drinking and driving through law was quite different from that of Norway and Sweden. On the one hand, Finland had not adopted the per se provisions of the laws in the other countries. The drinking-and-driving offense was defined in classical terms, stated in the 1937 law as driving "when drunk or under the influence of alcohol."

On the other hand, penalties for the offense in Finland were draconian. Under the 1937 law, the maximum penalty had been set at two years' imprisonment. In 1950, this penalty was doubled to four years, with provisions for six years' imprisonment in the event that bodily injury was caused and seven years in the event that death was caused through the prohibited behavior. In 1957, the maximum penalty in the event of a crash producing death was raised to eight years. Actual sentences also were severe, typically three to six months' imprisonment, which is a considerable multiple of the typical sentences meted out in Norway and Sweden. Furthermore, convicted Finns were punished with loss of the driver's license for two to three years, with permanent revocation on the second offense.

In the course of a visit to Scandinavia in 1974, I obtained Finnish traffic statistics, permitting an interrupted time-series analysis of the effects of the doubling of the maximum penalty in 1950, an act that might be expected to have altered public perceptions of the severity of punishment for drinking and driving (see Ross 1975, pp. 303-308).

Motor-vehicle fatalities in Finland per 10,000 vehicles registered are graphed in figure 6-1, which shows a sharp subsequent decline that reaches a borderline level of statistical significance. The decline is even clearer in data on crash-related injuries, presented in figure 6-2. That drop is statistically significant—that is, it is very likely not the result of the instabil-

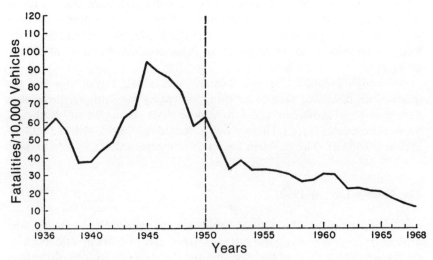

Source: Ross (1975).

Figure 6-1. Motor-Vehicle Fatalities in Finland per 10,000 Registered Vehicles, 1936-1968 (1940-1945 Registrations Estimated)

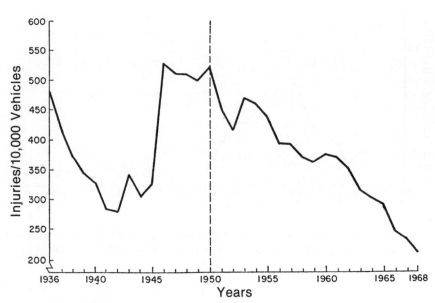

Source: Ross (1975).

Figure 6-2. Injuries in Motor-Vehicle Crashes in Finland per 10,000
Registered Motor Vehicles, 1936-1968 (1940-1945 Registrations
Estimated)

ity of the curve (the conclusion of significance is contingent on disregarding
the pre-1946 data).

However, various considerations militate against ascribing the change
in these figures, even if significant, to the 1950 law. One such consideration
is the fact that the change in the level of the series is greater for injuries than
for fatalities, which is unexpected because alcohol is more often involved in
fatalities. Another consideration is that there is little drop—in fact, there is
a diminution of the general downward slope—in the curve of single-vehicle
fatalities diagramed in figure 6-3. These fatalities are more likely to involve alcohol than fatalities in general. The decline was considerably greater
in the curve of multiple-vehicle fatalities, not shown here, where less alcohol
involvement and therefore less deterrence by drinking-and-driving laws
would have been expected. In short, if there were a nonrandom decline in
Finnish crashes in 1950, there would be no justification for characterizing it
as a product of the drinking-and-driving law. In this instance, at least, a
marked increase in the severity of threatened punishment for violation of a
drinking-and-driving law did not have observable deterrent consequences.

As a footnote to the Finnish experience, it might be noted that although
the maximum penalty was doubled in 1950, actual penalties meted out by
judges did not increase. Rather, 1950 represented a turning point in the pro-

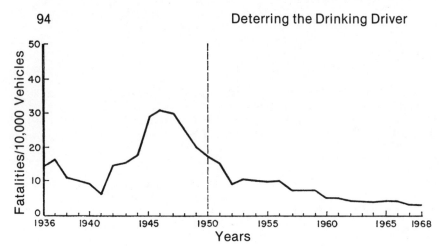

Source: Ross (1975).
Figure 6-3. Single-Vehicle Crash Fatalities in Finland per 10,000
Registered Vehicles, 1936-1968 (1940-1945 Registrations
Estimated)

portion of long sentences (six months or more), which had been increasing
until that time but which steadily declined thereafter, from more than 60
percent in 1950 to less than 10 percent in the mid-1960s (Ross 1976). The
reasons for this change are not known, but they may include an unwill-
ingness of judicial personnel to accept the legislative mandate.

The Chicago Crackdown

An evaluated severity crackdown occurred when Chicago Judge Raymond
Berg attempted to increase penalties received by convicted drinking drivers.
As supervising judge of Chicago's traffic court, Berg decreed that, during
the period around Christmas 1970, all people convicted of drinking and
driving would receive automatic seven-day jail sentences. The program
subsequently was extended for six months because of its presumed success.
A "remarkable automobile safety record" was claimed by comparing
Christmas of 1970 with previous years on the criterion of police-reported
fatalities and injuries "involving alcohol" (Field 1971).

However, submission of crash data from Chicago to interrupted time-
series analysis led to the conclusion that the lower crash-related-fatality rate
in December 1970 was not significant—that is, it could not be distinguished
from chance variation (Robertson, Rich, and Ross 1973). Moreover, data
from Milwaukee, chosen as a comparison city because of similar location
and climate but no change in the treatment of drinking drivers, showed an
even greater proportional decrease at the time than the Chicago data,

although again the decrease was not significant. The study concluded that the Chicago crackdown was not effective in deterring drinking and driving.

One possible cause of this failure is the fact that the judicial threat was not fulfilled in practice. Law-enforcement files reveal that although police arrested more than 1,100 drivers per month for drinking-and-driving offenses during the first six months of 1971, the total number of seven-day jail sentences for all traffic offenses during the entire period was only 557.

One unanticipated side effect of the Chicago crackdown was a decline in the proportion of convictions for charges of drinking and driving. This decline was experienced primarily among drivers who had not been tested for blood alcohol (implied consent not being accepted in Illinois law at the time). Perhaps one can see in this an example of the legal system's accommodating where possible to pressures to shield offenders from sanctions considered to be unusually severe. The failure of judges to follow through with threatened jail sentences in cases of convictions furnishes another example of this tendency. Where tests of bodily substances gave objective evidence of an illegal concentration of alcohol in the blood, the pressure to shield offenders apparently was successfully resisted.

Traffictown Gets Tough on Drinking Drivers

Another glimpse of the effects of judicial action to increase the severity of penalties for drinking and driving is offered by Traffictown (not its real name), a city of 30,000 people in New South Wales (Misner and Ward 1975). The local magistrate in Traffictown obtained notoriety for his tough penalties in drinking-and-driving cases, and he was in fact far more likely than his predecessor or other magistrates in the region to hand down formal convictions of the accused and to penalize with unusually high fines.

The report on Traffictown finds that serious crashes did not drop perceptibly during the judge's campaign, but several interesting and unexpected side effects were indicated. There was a decrease in total reported crashes, very likely indicating that drivers involved in minor crashes failed to report these in order to avoid possible court appearances. The average value of insurance claims also increased, a fact possibly explicable by the suppression of reports of minor crashes in order to avoid contact with the judge. Furthermore, proportions of crash-involved drivers charged by the police dropped significantly even though the crashes that came to police attention were, on the average, more serious. This fact implicates the police in the effort to avoid the judge.

Such effects are understandable if we assume that reporters and prosecutors of violations regarded the judicial campaign as excessive and acted to shield themselves and others from exposure to it. This assumption is plausible for the case at hand and was in fact noted by Misner and Ward: "Traffictown drivers considered traffic laws retributive, rather than a deterrent to dangerous driving. Only when traffic violations result in injury were heavy penalties considered appropriate" (p. 679). An important consequence of this situation was that the judge's toughness in punishing offenders appearing before him resulted in others' apparently avoiding the experience of any punishment at all.

Conclusion

The experiences reported here do not support the deterrence model in the matter of severity of penalty. It could not be demonstrated that the increase in the statutory severity of sanctions in Finland, the increase in the threat of judicial severity in Chicago, or the increase in actual judicial severity in Traffictown produced declines in indexes of the threatened behavior. However, conclusions about severity based on these cases must be qualified by the knowledge that the drinking-and-driving offense is one for which the general level of certainty of punishment is extremely low.

I suggest that there may well be interaction between severity and certainty—that if the probability of punishment is so low as to be negligible, then severity of the threatened punishment cannot be expected to influence behavior. The studies reviewed here in their cumulative impact justify the policy recommendation to avoid dependence on severe penalties in attempting to cope with drinking and driving, at least as long as the probability of an offender's being apprehended remains very low. Given the plausibility of the interaction explanation in these instances, I do not think that these results are overly damaging to a sophisticated theory of deterrence but that they remind us of the need for subtlety and complexity in our theoretical statements.

The other lesson to be learned from these experiences is that penalties considered unusually severe are unlikely to be forthrightly applied and that they may generate unexpected and undesired side effects when the attempt to apply them is made. Underlying the intellectual order of black-letter law is a social order of legal actors, and these can be expected to resist innovations that overturn established ways of doing things, especially when such innovations are considered extreme and unfair. This point has been noted elsewhere—for example, in discussion of the fact that the relatively common death sentences meted out in the United Kingdom in the late eighteenth and early nineteenth centuries were seldom carried out:

> Most people thought the death penalty tended to promote crime, believing it did not deter the criminal, who regarded it as a risk of the calling. . . but

that it did deter the prosecutor, magistrate, jury and judge, who were tempted to strain the law to avoid the risk of what was felt to be an unjust penalty. [Tobias 1968, p. 200]

The same point is made by the contemporary criminologist, James Q. Wilson, observing the mundane plea bargain:

[T]he more severe the penalty, the more unlikely that it will be imposed. . . . [P]rosecutors and judges will try to get a guilty plea, and all they can offer in return is a lesser sentence. The more severe the sentence, the greater the bargaining power of the accused, and the greater the likelihood that he will be charged with a lesser offense. Extremely long mandatory minimum sentences do not always strengthen the hand of society; they often strengthen the hand of the criminal instead. [1975, p. 179]

There are many points of discretion in the application of legal sanctions, and deformations may occur. For example, police may reduce arrests in a particular category, prosecutors may fail to charge in the category, judges and juries may fail to convict or find reason to mitigate the penalties, and those convicted may find ways to avoid the prescribed sanctions. As I suggested in an earlier paper, "If levels of actual punishment are to rise as intended, it may be necessary for the law-giver simultaneously to limit the discretion of legal actors and reduce their ability to resist the initiated change. Bearing in mind the complexity of the legal system and the manifold points of discretion, this is no simple order" (Ross 1976, p. 412).

7 Conclusion

This chapter reviews the findings of the literature survey concerning law and the deterrence of drinking and driving and attempts to interpret these findings as they address the validity of the deterrence model. My intent is to indicate the progress that has been made and the gaps that remain in our knowledge and to suggest some possibilities for improving the ways in which legal policy addresses the problem of drinking and driving.

A Lost Literature on Deterrence

In discussing the evidence on deterrence to be gained from the ASAP experience, Franklin Zimring has referred to a " 'lost experiment,' a program invisible to the social science community concerned with deterrence" (1978, p. 155). I believe that Zimring underestimated the extent of the loss by commenting only on a single set of experiences and data. The traffic-law literature is indeed a vast mine of comparable experience and information, one that has been almost untapped by the academic community, even in these days of enormous concern about the capabilities and limitations of law in influencing behavior. This is regrettable since the floods of correlational analyses based on official statistics, victim surveys, and similar data on conventional crimes have largely been relegated to the dust heap after recognition of their inherent methodological problems (Blumstein, Cohen, and Nagin 1978; Cook 1977).

Traffic-law innovations have been neglected by established criminologists partly because much of the reported research is applied research. It often originates in agencies that are primarily mission oriented and interested in the resolution of specific questions arising from local circumstances. The research sometimes is marked by "quick and dirty" procedures and, what is worse, is sometimes tainted by the need of officials out on a limb—"trapped administrators"—to find positive results to support their existing investments and commitments (Campbell 1969).

The field is also prone to self-serving conclusions on the part of vested interests other than the traditional political ones. Builders of highways and vehicles are eager to see the blame for crashes laid squarely on the "nut behind the wheel"—in the case of drinking drivers, the "killer drunk"

(Gusfield 1981). Those charged with controlling these dangerous deviants are not entirely opposed to this characterization since it may help obtain more resources for often underfinanced programs.

An occasional consequence of the applied focus of the research is methodological inadequacy. Some people with a strong interest in traffic policy are inadequately trained in social-science methodology and statistics. They may lack appreciation of their own limitations as well as access to the knowledge needed to capitalize on research possibilities that their administrative powers might permit. Furthermore, a good proportion of even the competently done studies is relatively inaccessible, appearing in the proceedings of technical meetings, in research-report series of state and national motor-vehicle and transportation departments, and in the publications of institutes and laboratories with limited mailing lists. Only one major research journal is published in the field.

Conversely, the opportunities provided in this field increasingly have been attracting trained researchers who have produced results measuring up to high standards of competence including methodological sophistication and policy neutrality. I refer not only to the work of isolated academicians in the field but also to that of organizations such as the California Department of Motor Vehicles and the safety-research centers at the University of Michigan and the University of North Carolina, not to mention the Insurance Institute for Highway Safety, which because of its fierce criticism of the products of the so-called safety establishment, has been careful to produce studies capable of withstanding critical barrages.

The problem of access to competent information has been further reduced by the availability of libraries such as the National Technical Information Service in Washington, D.C., and (for materials on drinking and driving) the publication of a series of abstracts at the University of California at Los Angeles. It is regrettable that the academic criminological community normally has not used these sources of valuable information.

Thus, a quantity of acceptable and accessible research in traffic safety now exists. Moreover, it exists in area of policy where there is a unique potential for understanding the operation of the legal system. One source of this potential is the very peculiarity of the traffic-law area; in much of its domain, traffic law is virtually the only important mechanism of social control present. Traffic-law violations are in many instances quintessential mala prohibita—acts that, in the absence of law, would violate no other social norms. Thus, the area offers the possibility for isolating the effect of legal factors from the customary and moral factors that usually accompany them and interfere with clear attributions of cause and effect.

Another source of the unique potential of traffic-law research is the presence of large volumes of data, sometimes of exceptional validity and reliability as social-data series go. Fatal crashes furnish a good example.

They are relatively clearly defined and well measured over time and across jurisdictions. Differences in their definition often can be minimized by application of empirically derived correction factors. Although in small jurisdictions fatal crashes can be quite variable due to the small size of the data bases, they can be related to larger data bases such as injury-producing crashes for confirmation. The agencies responsible for traffic gather crash and other statistics routinely and in considerable detail, and with the advent of computerized files they are able to produce complex and precise indexes (the U.S. Department of Transportation is currently engaged in programs designed greatly to increase the quality of data on both fatal and nonfatal crashes). Drinking and driving, the example at hand, can be indexed rather well by looking at refined crash series such as those involving single vehicles during nighttime hours.

A further matter to note about research on traffic law is that the area generates numerous policy innovations, permitting close and detailed studies of legal change in a variety of situations. Replication and cumulation of research are possible in this area as in few others of legal studies. Furthermore, the moral neutrality and penal triviality of some aspects of traffic law have allowed studies with classical experimental designs in an area where these are exceptionally rare because of ethical and practical difficulties (see, for example, Blumenthal and Ross 1973; Ross and Blumenthal 1975; Klein 1981).

I believe these considerations point to the suitability and importance of attention to traffic-law research on the part of the general criminological community and especially students of deterrence. After conceding the existence of problems and inadequacies in some of the literature, I believe that inattention to the balance of the literature is due partly to ignorance (unfamiliarity with a somewhat obscure literature) and partly to bias (a sharing in academic circles of the lawyer's view that traffic violations are trivial, traffic courts corrupt, and traffic bureaucracy incompetent). Contempt on the part of lawyers, trained and paid as they traditionally are, for problems that are individually small though significant as a group is understandable, but this view ought not to be adopted by social scientists concerned with explaining ordinary and everyday behavior.

Drinking and driving as a cause of serious traffic crashes is a major social problem, and its study is unquestionably worthwhile from the viewpoint of policy implementation. As summarized by the Insurance Institute for Highway Safety:

> A public health problem of staggering proportions, in terms of both damage to human health and economic waste, is confronting the nation today. By 1975, motor vehicle crash injuries, conservatively estimated, were costing the nation more than $14 billion annually, including the cost of emergency medical aid, hospital care, rehabilitation, lost wages, and other direct and indirect costs. These costs exceed $20 billion today.

Of the leading causes of death to Americans, motor vehicle crash injuries
are second only to cancer in their economic burden. They are accounting
for about 52,000 deaths a year. They account for the majority of new cases
of paraplegia and quadraplegia. They are the single leading cause of severe
facial lacerations and fractures. They contribute prominently to new cases
of epilepsy and brain damage. They kill more Americans ages 1-35 than any
other cause. [1981, p. 1]

Drinking and driving is a particularly apt field in which to study the
abilities and limitations of law in affecting behavior and, in particular, the
deterrence model. The keys to this field's importance are the numbers of
policy innovations that permit evaluation and the existence of many
available data sources that index the prevalence of drinking and driving,
especially fatal crashes and more-refined series like crashes on weekend
nights. The routine nature of the data-gathering enterprise protects these
series against problems of instrumentation in the usual case and makes
powerful interrupted time-series analyses and other quasi-experimental
studies feasible at very little cost. With the growing availability of appropriate computerized statistical models for these studies, the promise in
this area of research for advances in the study of deterrence is very bright.

The current review covers an international literature of varied quality.
Some of the innovations, like the Norwegian law of 1936, are problematic
because the data gathered at the time were not up to today's standards in
terms of completeness or detail. Some innovations were introduced at
especially unfortunate times for the purpose of analysis; this includes the
Dutch law, the Victorian law, and the U.S. ASAPs, in addition to the
Swedish law of 1941. In nearly all cases there is some reason to doubt the extent to which the law in action was affected by the formal policy innovations, and even many of the formal innovations appear less radical in
retrospect than they seemed at the time. However, a review of these related
policy innovations in a wide variety of settings has the benefit of cumulating
knowledge. It leads to conclusions that can now be accepted as plausible
scientific generalizations.

What Has Been Learned

I believe that in this survey I have covered the entire available literature on
attempts to reduce drinking and driving through increments in the threatened legal punishment where these have been accompanied by reasonably
competent evaluations. I have also noted additional innovations reputed to
have been effective even where the evidence is scientifically flawed. I believe
that this information justifies the following conclusions:

1. Changes in the law promising increased certainty or combined certainty and severity of punishment reduce the amount of drinking and driv-

ing. The U.K. experience of 1967 remains the best demonstration of this, as it resulted in a statistically significant decline in serious crashes that was shown to be particularly strong in drinking hours and not apparent in non-drinking hours. The extent of this effect also seems to have been greater in the United Kingdom than in other countries where similar deterrence programs were adopted. The British law was the most newsworthy and notable of those studied and therefore most likely to achieve changes in perception of the threat, although little direct evidence is available concerning public perceptions. Apparently less effect was achieved in some cases where the formal legal change was equivalent but public notice was less, as at the inception of the New Zealand legislation. However, the United Kingdom does not seem to have been an isolated case. France, the Netherlands, and Canada offer evidence of the generality of the deterrent effect of laws following the Scandinavian model. Even some of the more-negative reports such as that from New Zealand were characterized by disappointingly small changes in effect measures rather than by a complete absence of favorable effects; in these cases a combination of gradual formal change and low visibility furnish explanations for a reduced effect consistent with the deterrence model. Moreover, there is strong support for the proposition that highly publicized enforcement campaigns effectively diminish fatal crashes. Again, the United Kingdom furnishes an excellent example, but others are found in Australia, New Zealand, and if one chooses to accept the final analysis, the U.S. ASAPs.

2. Changes in behavior resulting from changes in the certainty of threat, on the order of those achieved by policy innovations to date, are evanescent. The reductions in the indicators of drinking and driving have disappeared after a few months or years, in the case of programs intended to be permanent, and closely upon termination of programs intended to be temporary. Loss of effect for the British Road Safety Act was formally proclaimed by official sources after a review of various data series including nighttime fatalities and blood-alcohol levels among drivers killed in crashes. Similar diminutions of effect are clear in all other studies that have reported long-term postintervention data. Some studies of limited campaigns have failed to report postcampaign data, but there is no reason to believe that they would have come to different results.

3. Innovations confined to manipulation of the severity of the legal punishment, without a concomitant change in its certainty, produce no effect on the apparent incidence of drinking and driving or its aftermath in crashes. In places like Traffictown and Chicago, the situation regarding drinking drivers did change but in unexpected and undesired ways. Increased severity of the prescribed punishment appears to result in changes that lessen the certainty of its application, which may in turn even reduce the deterrent effectiveness of the law.

4. In the study of the applicability of the deterrence model to drinking and driving, as with traditional criminality, virtually no evidence illustrates, one way or the other, the effect of celerity or swiftness of punishment. Although there has been some concern in policy circles with increasing the celerity of punishment (for example, the ASAPs' attempts to deal with bottlenecks in the processing of accused drinking drivers), celerity has never in reported cases been manipulated in the absence of changes affecting certainty and severity.

The Deterrent Influence of Law on Behavior

My purpose in this section is to offer a more-detailed interpretation of the findings concerning deterrence that have come out of the literature on drinking-and-driving law. At this point it is necessary to engage in more speculation than in the balance of the book, due to the nature of the evidence. Typically, we know that a program was undertaken to increase the severity or certainty of the legal threat for drinking and driving, and we may have evidence that such a program was put into effect. We also may know that some effort was made to publicize the program, although information often is lacking or very sketchy. Some studies provide evidence of the extent which a program became known in a jurisdiction, although very rarely is there any information on the degree of perception of the legal threat. There is also very seldom direct evidence of changes in drinking and driving, as would be provided by competent roadside-sample surveys using screening breath tests. More commonly, statistics on crashes and casualties are presented as indirect evidence of drinking-and-driving behavior. The latter series are, of course, direct evidence of the ultimate policy goals being achieved, and especially when refined (for example, limited to fatalities at night), they are good, although not perfect, indicators of the intermediate goals to which the deterrence model points.

Let us consider the three components of the deterrence model and ask the extent to which their causal influence has been tested and demonstrated in the world literature on drinking-and-driving laws. Before commencing this exercise we would do well to note that the studies being considered furnish instances of marginal increases in one or more of the components of the model, not of the absolute introduction of legal threats. All instances in which the drinking-and-driving law followed the Scandinavian model occured in legal systems that previously had proscribed and threatened the behavior in question. Indeed, many of the innovations appear to have been small steps in a series of changes bringing classical laws into conformity with the Scandinavian model—for example, changing the nature of a specified blood-alcohol concentration from a presumption of alcohol influence to a per se violation. Thus, the literature investigates increments in levels of deterrence variables—not their presence or absence—and negative results must be understood as appropriately limited in implication.

We may begin the exercise by noting that the literature is unenlightening in the matter of perceived celerity of punishment. Few programs were established with much concern for celerity—some of the ASAPs were an exception—and none attempted to measure changes in its perception. Moreover, the increases experienced in celerity invariably were associated with other changes relevant to the deterrence model and would thus be difficult to disentangle. (Of course, the criminologist will recognize this picture in the literature of traditional crime as well). Celerity is an orphan variable in deterrence research. Although the Scandinavian model for drinking-and-driving law embodies measures that might be expected to increase celerity—notably, the administrative lifting of the driver's license before final judgment—its achievements in these efforts have not been assessed.

More information is available on perceived severity of threat in the drinking-and-driving literature, and it is not favorable to this component of the deterrence model. Innovations limited to increasing only the severity of punishment seem to be associated with little or no change in the indicators of drinking and driving, but rather with unforeseen and disturbing changes in the functioning of the legal system. However, the literature on drinking-and-driving-law innovations encounters increases of severity only in situations where the certainty of punishment is extremely low. Since it is reasonable to expect some interaction between these variables, the negative findings on severity must be understood as limited to extremely low levels of certainty as a background condition.

Considerable evidence shows the positive effect of increments in perceived certainty of punishment due to the introduction of Scandinavian-type laws and as a consequence of enforcement campaigns. Publicized and newsworthy interventions designed to increase the actual probabilities of punishment for drinking and driving seem almost always to be accompanied by corresponding declines in the variables indicating this behavior. However, in the long run the declines are countered by tendencies to return to the status quo ante, whether or not the increased actual probabilities of detection, conviction, and punishment are maintained. This fact requires further explanation.

In my opinion, the key lies in the very modest level of real threat that current drinking-and-driving laws are able to produce. This fact is noted for the United States by Jones and Joscelyn:

> Research suggests that a driver in the U.S. would have to commit some 200 to 2,000 DWI [driving while under the influence] violations to be caught, after which he would still stand only a 50-50 chance of being punished—mildly at that. Such a risk is apparently acceptable even to most social drinkers, who are able to control their drinking. [1978, p. 56]

Estimates of the probability of apprehension given here are based on those of Borkenstein (1975) for the probability of arrest in routine policing and of Beitel, Sharp, and Glauz (1975) for the probability in Kansas City during the ASAP while driving on patrolled roads. Similar low levels of actual threat have been reported in other countries. Persson (1978, p. 112) estimates chance of apprehension in Sweden at less than 1 in 200; in New Zealand, Lonsdale and Stacey (1981, p. 15) cite a figure of about 1 in 1,000.

Another way to appreciate the level of actual threat under conditions of normal policing is suggested by figure 7-1, in which Summers and Harris

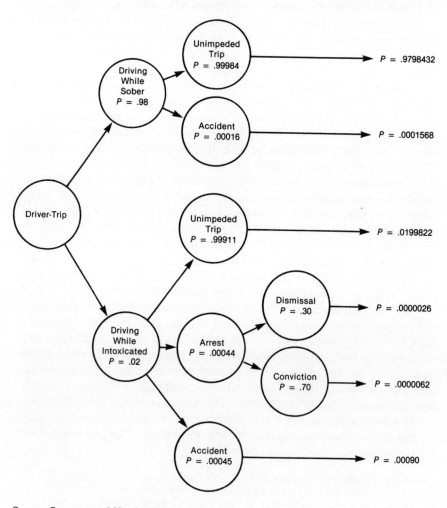

Source: Summers and Harris 1978, p. 10.

Figure 7-1. Probabilities of Driver-Trip Outcomes

(1978) diagram the conditional probabilities of arrest and accident when driving while sober or under the influence of alcohol. The figure shows that the probability of an accident when driving under the influence (0.00045), although three times the comparable probability when sober (0.00016), is nonetheless miniscule. The probability of arrest (0.00044) is of the same order. The probability of an impeded trip while impaired is thus less than 1/1,000. To increase the chance of any impediment to the trip to as much as, say 1/100, would require more than a twentyfold increase in the probability of arrest.

In routine circumstances, the perceived risk of apprehension for traffic offenses, including drinking and driving, is considerably overestimated (Cohen 1978; Norström 1981; McEwen and McGuire, 1981). It is likely that the introduction of novel laws and campaigns described in this report have resulted in even more-exaggerated estimations of punishment certainty. In light of the actual changes in enforcement attached to most of these innovations, I find it hard to think of anything other than gross misperception of the threat that would warrant important changes in the subject behavior through deterrence. Unfortunately, the perception of threat as a function of interventions is not well documented in the literature, and this interpretation has to be considered speculative. It is supported by its reasonableness in explaining both the apparent response of drinking and driving to the initiation of these laws and campaigns and the gradual falling off of the apparent effect in those instances in which the enforcement change was intended to be permanent. It helps to interpret the paradox found in the United Kingdom, France, and other places of a long-term decline in the deterrent effect of the law simultaneous with continued increases in the actual probability of apprehension as expressed by numbers of screening tests, charges, and convictions.

In short, the deterrent effect of Scandinavian-type laws and enforcement campaigns apparently is due to an exaggerated perception of the probability of apprehension of violators. This exaggeration can be explained by the publicity and media attention accompanying these innovations. The more spectacular the publicity and attention, the greater the reported effect of the law. Laws that meet the most critical resistance, as in the United Kingdom, seem to have been the most successful in their initial deterrence of drinking and driving.

These speculations help to make sense of the data on attempts to increase severity. Among the reasons for the failure of severity of penalty to deter drinking and driving may well be the interaction of certainty of punishment and severity. At very low levels of certainty, any amount of penalty can be dismissed. This interpretation also explains why, beyond the question of legal deterrence, drivers seem to be willing to accept impressive multiplications of the risks of death and injury by combining drinking and driving. In parallel fashion, one might expect that successful attempts to increase certainty of apprehension would yield no deterrence if severity were minimal.

A reasonable interpretation of the results of this review is that introductions of Scandinavian-type laws and enforcement campaigns have led to high levels of perceived certainty of punishment on the part of potential violators. Because of publicity and media attention, these perceptions were grossly exaggerated when compared with the actual probabilities of apprehension and conviction. Since the real risks increased more moderately, the deterrent accomplishment rested not on a firm foundation but rather on a temporary scaffold that became undermined through experience. The driver on the highway learned that, in an unintentional and well-meant fashion, his government was engaged in deception.

Matters of Ignorance

It is obvious from the speculative nature of parts of this chapter that more needs to be known about the function of the components of legal threat in affecting the behavior of drinking and driving. A major question, and the center of my speculation, concerns the relationship between actual and perceived certainty, severity, and celerity of punishment (Gibbs 1975). I find it surprising that in all the published evaluations of Scandinavian-type legal innovations there has not been a systematic study of initial levels of perceived threat and changes in these levels corresponding with the specific innovations. This would best be approached by periodic polls of successive random samples of the driving population over a prolonged baseline period, as well as during and after operations.

More also needs to be known about the interaction among components of the deterrence model, especially the relationship between certainty and severity. One of the missed opportunities of the ASAP experiences was the possibility of systematically varying increments in order to test for joint and interactive effects. Short of such a major operation, it would be worthwhile to divide future implementations of increased threat into phases, introducing changes in certainty and severity at different times. This would permit interrupted time-series analyses of marginal increases in one component accompanied by stability in the other, followed by a period of joint increase (the timing and order of component changes should of course be varied from case to case).

The question of a threshold for the operation of certainty of threat is important for policy as well as theory. The practical usefulness of a deterrence policy is limited by the amount of enforcement resources that are likely to be allocated and by any undesirable side effects that an intensive patrol for drinking drivers might involve. Perhaps the crucial experiment here would involve raising the level of actual certainty of apprehension to the bounds of political and financial possibility.

Deterrence as Policy

If one poses the question, Does deterrence work in the area of drinking and driving?, the answer would differ (assuming present levels of threat and in the present state of knowledge) according to whether the short term or the long term is meant. This review of the literature shows that deterrence works in the short term. Adoptions of Scandinavian-style laws and enforcement campaigns based on such laws provide many convincing examples of the ability of legal threat to control behavior in this area and to achieve the ultimate result of a decline in casualties. Regardless of the fact that many drinking drivers may be problem drinkers, and that some observers have posited that problem drinkers are not deterrable, the deterrence efforts studied here have had effects. Furthermore, and again in the short run, the savings attained have most likely exceeded the costs of these programs.

However, the long-run prognosis for achieving marginal increases in deterrence through modifications in existing law is less positive. Even the most successful of deterrent interventions appear in the course of a few years to have lost their entire beneficial effects. My interpretation of these facts is that the level of threat achieved in adoptions of the Scandinavian model has been too low to maintain important effects over time. Moreover, we do not know what level, if any, of certainty and severity of threat will suffice to maintain deterrence of drinking and driving.

Surely research is needed to vouch for the possibility of long-run deterrence and, what is more, to give a clearer indication of its price, not only in terms of police cars and salaries but also in terms of exposure of the population to oppressive surveillance. I am not willing to accept the conclusion that Scandinavian-type drinking-and-driving laws require oppressive surveillance to maintain deterrence but rather believe that applied research should explore this possibility.

Deterrence may in some circumstances be a feasible and cost-effective legal policy. Present knowledge provides some guidance as to how we might achieve maximum effects from deterrence strategies; if crucial experiments are to be done, the laws to be investigated should be guided by this knowledge. A first point to be made is that very likely existing levels of severity should not be increased. Indeed, the mere retraction of the driver's license for a few weeks might be a noticeable and presumably effective threat in an automobile-dependent society. Recourse to heavy fines and mandatory jail sentences seems likely to encourage deformations in the legal system, such as police leniency or even corruption, plea bargaining, and increased findings of not guilty. These adjustments may have the unintended effect of reducing the certainty of punishment and diminishing rather than increasing the total deterrent effect of the law. It may be true that many drivers continue to drive illegally with suspended licenses, thus presenting a challenge to the authority of the legal system. However, the question from the general-deterrence viewpoint is whether license suspension is feared and not whether it works well as an incapacitative device.

The accumulated knowledge in this area indicates that an important element of a deterrence-based program is the presentation to drinking drivers of a subjectively important chance of apprehension should they commit the violation. Experience shows that it is possible to increase patrol for drinking and driving and to raise the apprehension rate considerably. Common sense further suggests that patrols should be deployed at times and places where the problem behavior is common—for example, on weekend nights and on roads with concentrations of taverns and restaurants. Indeed, when police are left to their own devices, they select this mode of patrol. Perhaps the most promising innovation on the U.S. scene would be to introduce some convincing threat of probable apprehension for the driver who believes (usually correctly) that he can drink and drive without giving cause for police to suspect him of the violation. Roadblock testing may be a means of accomplishing this, if the roadblocks appear to be frequent. These would probably be constitutional if performed on the basis of checks of papers or vehicles, as in Canada and Norway, during which the odor of alcoholic beverages would justify a screening test for blood alcohol. Another model is furnished by the British legislation, which makes the occurrence of a traffic violation or crash the equivalent of reasonable cause for a police officer to suspect the presence of alcohol and to demand an appropriate screening test. Under this legislation it is possible to engage in a massive testing, as was the case during the Cheshire blitz.

The issue of swiftness or celerity of punishment, although disregarded in research, should receive attention in future legal innovations. One way in which punishment could be made to follow more closely upon the violation would be to abandon the criminal definition of drinking and driving, at least in routine cases and for first offenses, making it a civil offense to be handled with dispatch by an administrative organization (see Jones, Joscelyn, and McNair 1979). Punishments such as imprisonment would not be applicable under this procedure, but for independent reasons such punishments are contraindicated. This change probably would have a positive effect on the certainty of the penalty as well. What is more, it would place the routine violation in a fitting legal category; as has been noted elsewhere (Force 1977; King and Tipperman 1975), one of the current law's major problems is its treatment of drivers as criminals when they are not believed by the public to warrant this designation. The health of the legal system would benefit from support of its workings by the citizenry. A variety of commentators have proposed legal modifications along these lines that promise to increase the deterrent effect of drinking-and-driving law (Little 1980, p. 269). These possibilities should be tried and the results studied.

Beyond Deterrence

To the policymaker confronted with the need to devise programs for reducing the drinking-and-driving problem, deterrence may be an appealing approach. Indeed, in the very short run, for a turnkey operation, deterrence-based policies may be the only available options. The research reviewed in this book supports the promise that deterrence can work in this time frame. Enforcement campaigns in jurisdictions with Scandinavian-type laws (and perhaps even in those that retain classical laws) are likely to produce savings in lives and injuries. Deterrence-based programs are far likelier to succeed than programs based on rehabilitation and treatment of offenders, partly because the latter are likely to be ineffective (see, for example, Nichols et al. 1978a; 1978b) and partly because even if effective they could be applied only to that small fraction of potential participants in crashes who become known to authorities. Deterrence, if effective, acts on the entire population of potential drinking drivers, whether or not their prior record has marked them as likely to become involved in crashes.

However, deterrence-based policies are questionable in the long run. No such policies have been scientifically demonstrated to work over time under conditions achieved in any jurisdiction. This fact does not mean that such policies are hopeless but rather that success—if achievable—probably will involve something other than what has been done in the past. On the basis of the evidence, it will not suffice to import further elements of the Scandinavian approach into other jurisdictions in the expectation that Norway and Sweden have the answers. Moreover, the option of merely increasing penalties for drinking and driving has been strongly discredited by experience to date. The most hopeful opportunities for further deterrent accomplishments would seem to lie in increasing the actual probabilities of apprehension and conviction of drinking drivers.

Experience does suggest some ways in which this might be done, although the weakest link in our procedure seems to be apprehension, which is inherently difficult in the case of alcohol-influenced driving. Many procedures that might increase the probability of apprehension are intrusive and objectionable, thus costly not only in dollars but also in political support. How much is the public willing to bear in terms of police budgets and submission to roadblocks and spot checks?

To the extent that deterrent results are achieved based merely on exaggerated fears of punishment, such results seem destined to disappear over time, and in the course of these experiences there is likely to be erosion of the citizens' trust in their governments. A reasonable suggestion, then, seems to be that policymakers determine a maximum tolerable investment in deterrence and attempt to raise the actual threat for law violators to the limit permitted by these resources. If long-range effects cannot be accomplished at this level, then perhaps the deterrence approach should be left to its present function in which those who are apprehended are the obvious (drunks) and the unlucky (killers).

This statement is based on practical considerations. It makes no sense to base policy on techniques that, if they are to work, entail intolerable costs. However, another problem with the deterrence approach troubles me—namely, whether the kind of punishment needed to be effective as a deterrent can be morally defended as a criminal sanction.

It has been observed (for example, by Packer 1968) that the limits of the criminal sanction are set not by its ability to deter but by its appropriateness to the moral culpability of the offender. This strikes me as an intuitively reasonable proposition. Even well-meant and beneficial rehabilitative sanctions ought not to be imposed on someone whose behavior is innocent. This brings us to the question of the moral culpability of the alcohol-influenced driver. While drinking and driving on the massive scale experienced by modern societies is associated with costly and tragic consequences, the individual trip impaired by alcohol is extremely unlikely to harm anyone. Fatal and injury-producing crashes are extremely rare events. According to Summers and Harris's (1978) estimates for the United States, the probability of a crash is three times higher for the impaired driver than for the sober one. Yet the absolute risk of a crash for the impaired driver still is only on the order of 1 in 1,000, and the risk of causing injury and death is of course considerably lower. A New Zealand writer has expressed the matter thus: "At present . . . road fatality rates a car could on average be driven around the world 400 times before a fatality would result, and more than 30 times before a serious personal injury could be expected" (Parsons 1978, p. 9). From this perspective, even a high multiple of actual risk may be regarded as negligible. The non-crash-involved driver apprehended for driving with an illegal blood-alcohol concentration would most likely have completed his trip without incident, except for police intervention. This fact is recognized, if not always formally, by dealers in symbols, such as appellate-court judges and legislators, then very often informally, by trial-court judges and defense lawyers. In his immensely thought-provoking book on the matter, Joseph Gusfield has noted:

> On the public level of law and the media of public communications [drinking and driving] is criminal behavior—easily perceived to be like other

crimes; on the working level of daily routine it is mostly undetected. When drinking-driving becomes a matter of enforcement attention, its existence is ambiguous and a matter of policy and social construction, largely responded to by fine. . . . As a matter of Law, drinking-driving is a criminal offense; as a matter of law it is not more than a traffic violation. [1981, pp. 132-133]

The drinking-and-driving offense represents a combination of two morally neutral or even beneficial activities that can have catastrophic consequences, but with an extremely low probability. Similar problems are raised in other areas of law—for instance, pollution and areas of safety regulation—although exact parallels are not evident.

The fundamental justice of the deterrence approach thus is seen to be an open question. The situation noted by Gusfield illustrates that Americans answer this question with ambivalence. The killer drunk gets his due, but in the vast majority of cases of alcohol-impaired driving, the prohibited behavior is not seen as warranting highly punitive sanctions. To center policy on a strategy based on such ambiguous sentiments presents problems going beyond those of practicality. Perhaps what sets the Scandinavians apart in this matter is that with their temperance tradition they have a less-ambiguous and more-negative view of the moral nature of alcohol use than most nations today, and consequently they have less difficulty in accepting the justice of the deterrence approach to controlling drinking and driving.

Since the practicality of deterrence in the long run is questionable and its justice arguable, other approaches to the reduction of death and injury related to drinking and driving ought to be considered by the policymakers charged with this task. The possibilities for ameliorating the problem of drinking and driving become clearer if the nature of the problem to be addressed is redefined. I suggest two definitions that can lead to promising options for policy: One sees the drinking-and-driving problem as part of the general problem of controlling alcohol use, and the other sees the problem as part of the general problem of controlling the consequences of traffic crashes.

If the problem being faced is controlling alcohol use, a variety of avenues other than deterrence comes to mind. These have recently been considered by a committee of the National Academy of Sciences, whose report offers a large number of specific suggestions for policy. Some of these suggestions are based on acceptance of the "single distribution theory," which the committee described as follows:

[A] general reduction in the availability of alcoholic beverages should reduce overall alcohol consumption for both moderate and heavy drinkers. Such a reduction, particularly to the extent that it involves very heavy drinkers, would in turn yield public health benefits. [Moore and Gerstein 1981, p. 66]

A specific recommendation of the committee is to raise the price of alcoholic beverages in order to reduce consumption, a measure that very likely would have road-safety benefits among others. Recommendations more specifically related to the drinking-and-driving issue stress the desirability of reducing the dispensation of alcoholic beverages to people especially prone to drink and drive and in situations where driving is a likely consequence. For instance, very young drivers are disproportionately likely to become involved in alcohol-related crashes. Studies of recent state laws that have raised or lowered drinking ages (for example, Wagenaar 1981; Williams et al. 1982) show important safety benefits to be achieved by making the legal drinking age as high as politically feasible. Measures to shift consumption from sites where driving is necessary to those where it is not also are indicated. For instance, license fees for drinking establishments might be made proportional to pedestrian traffic and disproportional to vehicular traffic in the immediate vicinity during drinking hours. Suggestions that can be offered only half-seriously are to prohibit licensed premises from providing parking spaces for their patrons, to tax provision of such spaces, and to prohibit street parking in the vicinity of taverns.

Although some of these measures may be politically unrealistic, governments should at least avoid actively encouraging drinking and driving. This can be taken to heart by policymakers whose governments are directly involved in the liquor-distribution business. An example of unconscionable public policy is provided by New Hampshire, which has constructed a huge liquor store, surrounded by acres of parking, directly on the main interstate highway linking its major cities and the Boston metropolitan area.

If the problem of drinking and driving is viewed as an aspect of the larger problem of controlling the consequences of motor-vehicle crashes, a whole host of alternative policies promises to be effective (Haddon 1980). We may be able to follow Joseph Little's advice "to forget about more severe laws and work for a safer environment for drunks to drive in (sturdier cars, safe highways)" (1980, p. 284). This is a very broad goal, and it has the advantage over dealing with more narrowly defined problems in being relevant to crashes with any number of causes. A vehicle and highway that are safe for an alcohol-influenced driver are also safe for a driver who has a heart attack, who dozes off, who drops his lighted cigarette on his lap, who fails to see a stop sign or a vehicle approaching from an unexpected angle, and so forth.

This perspective has marked the efforts of the National Highway Traffic Safety Administration since its founding and has led to innovations such as provision of seat belts in vehicles, modification of fixed hazards on highways, and other programs with clearly cost-effective results. Although some of these innovations have at times been resisted on libertarian grounds, I believe they very likely are less instrusive than the operations that a workable and permanent deterrence-based program aimed at drinking drivers might entail. Being nonpunitive, they also avoid the moral problems inherent in the deterrence approach.

Moreover, a shift of concentration from the drinking driver to crash-related-damage reduction permits reliance on technological devices rather than on influencing individual behavior. As stated by Lily Hoffman, in connection with the example of automobile design:

> What technology has uniquely to offer to the solution of complex problems is a kind of option-reducing potential—the possibility of at least removing the decision from the individual (whom we have failed to change time and time again) to the societal level. [1973, p. 101]

One of the general lessons from the social-scientific study of law is that effects usually are easier to obtain from laws directed at a small, controllable number of organizational entities than from laws directed at masses of individuals. For instance, desegregation in housing is obtained by edicts directed to housing developers and authorities, taxes are most easily collected through withholding by employers, schools enforce the innoculation of children, and seat belts are installed in vehicles because of rules directed at manufacturers (and they lose their efficacy in part because individual behavior controls their use). Safety efforts achievable through manipulation of the vehicle or the road usually are imposed by this most efficacious type of law.

If the problem we are facing is that of reducing injuries and deaths associated with crashes, I am tempted to agree with Hoffman that "the safety car concept of passenger packaging can be seen as a kind of ultimate loss reductive solution" (1973, p. 101). However, until such time as this ultimate solution is available to the public, the possibilities inherent in the deterrence of drinking and driving should not be discarded. The accumulated research reviewed here testifies to the achievability of loss reduction in the short run through vigorous enforcement of laws following the Scandinavian model, although no evidence currently is available concerning the potential for achievement in the long run. The review does indicate some promising modifications of existing deterrence-based law. In the present state of the world, there is reason to adopt and evaluate these modifications, which may yield important interim benefits while the ultimate solution is awaited.

Afterword:
Recent U.S.
Developments

In the past two years numerous efforts have been made in U.S. jurisdictions to deal with drunk driving through deterrence-based laws. This deluge of legislation can be credited to the anti-drunk-driving movement—including such organizations as MADD and RID—which has responded to the problem of deaths and injuries associated with alcohol-impaired driving by a program centered on deterrence. The recent report of the Presidential Commission on Drunk Driving (1983) noted that in the previous year,[39] states had enacted "improved" legislation, and that "[l]egislators, enforcement officials, prosecutors, and judges around the country have responded to society's demands by enacting more effective legislation, apprehending more offenders, effectively prosecuting offenders, and meting out more appropriate sanctions."

Many of these efforts are being evaluated, adding to our knowledge of the capabilities and limitations of the deterrent approach. The implications of this recent American experience for the argument of the previous chapters will be discussed in this concluding note, prepared especially for the paperback edition. In general, it can be said that recent experience confirms that well-publicized punitive threats reduce the amount of drunk driving in the short run, though more severe penalties generate costly ripples in the criminal-justice system without a clear demonstration of safety benefits.

Certainty of Punishment

A major enforcement crackdown on drunk drivers was launched in the city of Stockton, California, between January 1976 and June 1979. It was inspired by the belief that the effective element in the Department of Transportation's ASAPs had been enforcement; the crackdown was funded by a grant from that agency. Ten extra police officers were assigned to drunk-driving patrol on Friday and Saturday nights, raising the estimated probability of apprehension for a drunk driver to about one chance in 300. This figure, though low in absolute terms, represents more than a tripling of the estimated normal risk in the United States and most other nations. The intensity of this crackdown is among the greatest in the literature and its duration was certainly the longest. Furthermore, a thorough evaluation was funded.

The evaluation of the Stockton crackdown (Voas and Hause 1983) found encouraging declines in nighttime crashes, when these were analyzed as an interrupted time series. Control series of daytime crashes and of pooled nighttime data from four comparable California cities did not show this effect. Moreover, a deterrent effect was noted through roadside sampling of drivers. There was a decline in the proportion of impaired drivers on weekend nights, from 8.8 percent in a baseline period to 5 percent after the project had been in operation for two years. The evaluation also found evidence that the weekend night patrol, although limited to selected sites, seemed to have affected crashes in the entire city. Moreover, although in action only on weekends there was a generalization of its effect to weekday nights as well. No changes were found in the number of crashes designated "alcohol-related" by the police, but this criterion is highly susceptible to instrumentation error and is properly discounted in the Stockton report.

As with other enforcement crackdowns, the Stockton data suggest that the deterrent effect achieved may not have survived the perceived termination of the project, even though the special patrol was continued on a reduced basis once Federal funds were cut off. Although the risk of apprehension for drunk drivers remained somewhat higher than before the crackdown, the project was perceived by the driving public as terminated. The enhanced but unpublicized threat could then be disregarded by those to whom it was addressed.

Apparent success of a deterrence-oriented program has also been reported in Albuquerque, New Mexico, where police were provided with convenient and versatile mobile breath-testing units. These "BAT Mobiles" were the subject of considerable commentary and media attention. They reduced the processing time for drunk-driving offenders from an average of 2 hours and 20 minutes to 20 to 25 minutes.

The Albuquerque evaluation (Woods and Calderwood 1982) noted that simultaneously with the provision of the new technology—and very likely at least partly in consequence of it—arrests of drunk drivers doubled within the city. The evaluators compared rates of fatal and injury crashes on Wednesday through Saturday nights with daytime crashes in Albuquerque and with nighttime crashes in other urban areas of the state. They concluded that five- to seven-percent declines in the crash rate were the effect of the BAT Mobile program and the consequent increase in risk of arrest for violators of the drunk-driving law. As the program became operational only at the end of 1979 it was not possible to appraise its long-term effects of this project.

Severity of Punishment

The most notable and common provision for increasing the severity of punishment for drunk drivers has been mandatory jail legislation. This is

currently in effect in 25 states, in many instances even for first-time offenders. Four jurisdictions providing mandatory jail for first-offender
drunk drivers were reviewed by the staff of the National Institute of Justice
(Gropper et al. 1983). This report will be summarized here.

In the State of Washington a one-day minimum jail sentence for first-
time drunk-driving offenders was instituted in 1980. Second offenders
received a mandatory 7-day minimum, and third offenders received a
90-day minimum jail term. It was found that drunk-driving charges by
police increased by about 25 percent between 1979, prior to the law, and
1982. In the first year following the new law, Seattle experienced a decrease
in fatal crashes from 68 to 60, an encouraging but probably not significant
change. The rate of "alcohol-related" traffic accidents reacted strangely:
they increased "substantially" in the first year and declined in the second
year. I believe that because of statistical and measurement deficiencies these
data are inadequate to evaluate the deterrent effect of the new law. However, the consequences of the legislation for the criminal-justice system are
better demonstrated. Findings of guilty on drunk-driving charges declined
from 80 percent before the law to 60 percent afterward. Deferred prosecutions rose from 1½ percent of cases to 12 percent. The jury trial rate
more than doubled. Failures to appear for trial went from 6 percent to 14
percent. Although those found guilty were, almost universally, sent to jail
(compared with fewer than 10 percent of offenders before the new law) the
criminal-justice system in its entirety became distorted in the direction of
freeing a large proportion of those charged, rather than applying the mandatory jail sentence. Furthermore, those convicted have imposed a heavy
burden on the system. Prosecutors and judges in Seattle estimated that they
spent about three-quarters of their time on drunk-driving cases; monthly
jail commitments increased more than tenfold in the first year and continued rising, and a new detention facility had to be opened to accom-
modate the flood of prisoners.

In passing, it might be noted that the Washington law has also been
found to be ineffective in changing the behavior of convicted drunk-driving
offenders. Salzberg and Paulsrude (1983), working in the Washington State
Department of Licensing, found that individuals convicted under the provisions of the 1980 mandatory jailing law had higher accident rates and
drunk-driving recidivism rates than those convicted under the prior law.

Somewhat comparable findings were reported for selected California
counties following passage of a provision for a 96-hour jail sentence for
first offenders in January 1982. (The California provision was not truly
mandatory, as judges were permitted to substitute treatment or probation.)
Highway Patrol arrests increased slightly following the inception of the new
law. In Los Angeles County, where drunk-driving arrests also increased
slightly, there was a slight increase in the number of violations charged.

But there were (1) a 10½-percent decrease in guilty pleas; (2) a 24-percent increase in jury trials for Group C misdemeanors (mainly drunk driving); and (3) a 10-percent decrease in such convictions. Trial delay increased dramatically: there was a 78-percent increase in continuances. Yet in almost three-quarters of convictions of first offenders, the judges refrained from imposing jail sentences, relying instead on fines, license restrictions, and probation (see also Los Angeles County Municipal Courts 1983).

Alameda County reported similar occurrences: large increases in representation of drunk-driving defendants by attorneys, increases in not-guilty pleas, in calendared jury trials, in time to sentencing, and in bench warrants issued because of nonappearance of defendants.

The California law was a complex intervention and its widespread publicity would lead one to expect increased perceived certainty of apprehension as well as severity of punishment. An analysis of crashes during the first nine months of the new law does provide evidence of a deterrent effect (Peck 1983). Using log-linear methods, the evaluator reported greater reductions in nighttime injury accidents than in daytime ones, and greater reductions in "had-been-drinking" fatal crashes than in the balance of fatal crashes. Issues of measurement validity constrain reliance on the latter finding, although the California practice of measuring blood alcohol in almost all drivers involved in fatal crashes makes this a better-than-usual comparison. The finding is confirmed by reductions in nighttime injury crashes, though not in fatalities, perhaps because of the small data base for the latter series. In any event, the preliminary report does suggest that the initial effect declined after three months, as experience elsewhere might lead one to predict. A final evaluation—using interrupted time-series methods—is promised, and should be instructive. However, the California law was complex, and other provisions pointed to an increased certainty of conviction. Therefore, a demonstration of its deterrent effectiveness could not unambiguously support the thesis that severity of threat was the cause. In contrast, distortions in the criminal-justice system can more confidently be attributed to the "tough" penalties of the law.

The National Institute of Justice report also describes events in Memphis, following a July 1982 Tennessee law providing a mandatory 48-hour jail sentence for first-offender drunk drivers. Unlike experience in the other jurisdictions mentioned, there were no increases in police charges, indictments, or trials. This is perhaps due to the lack of "any sustained public awareness campaign surrounding the law." Judges did apply the penalty nearly universally, severely effecting probation and correctional facilities. No data were presented on crashes. Because of the limited publicity it may be most reasonable to presume that Tennessee was not able to effect drivers' perceptions of the severe penalties in the law and was therefore unlikely to achieve deterrent effects.

In Cincinnati, prior to a 1983 revision of Ohio law, the experience of local toughness in handling drunk drivers revealed substantial impacts on correctional facilities, but no crash data for evaluating deterrence were presented.

In sum, these new experiences provide ambiguous support for the deterrent effect of severe penalties on drunk driving. They do, however, suggest that a high price may be paid for such provisions in the form of lowering conviction rates while increasing the burden on the personnel and facilities of the criminal-justice system.

Swiftness of Punishment

Experience until recently had not produced cases in which swiftness of punishment was manipulated in such a way that evaluation could determine its deterrent efficacy. Recent provisions for administrative license suspension come closer to providing such a test.

Drivers greatly fear license suspension, but its imposition has traditionally been conditioned on a judicial finding of guilt, such as for drunk driving or failure to provide a required breath test. In the United States, a person accused of the offense may easily perceive such an outcome to be far in the future and indefinitely postponable through the manipulations of competent defense counsel. This punishment seems to lack the advantage of swiftness. Of course, the conviction, in addition to being deferred, may also be perceived as improbable, compromising the certainty of punishment as well. Administrative license suspension changes the situation by providing that police may take the license on the spot from a driver who refuses a mandatory breath test or who fails it and can be charged with drunk driving. To comply with Constitutional principles, when this is done a permit is issued granting driving privileges for a limited period, during which the driver may appeal the police action to an administrative board. Unless the case is won at this hearing, the license is lost and punishment ensues. Importantly, the criterion at the administrative hearing is not the criminal one of proof beyond a reasonable doubt, but the civil one of preponderance of evidence, rendering success of appeals at this level generally remote. Of course, the license denial can subsequently be appealed to a court, but the delay—which under traditional laws postpones the punishment—under administrative license suspension can have the effect of continuing the punishment.

In 1976, Minnesota passed the first state law providing for administrative license suspension. This law was strengthened by amendment in July 1982 to discourage dilatory appeals. Similar laws were passed by an additional 17 states between 1981 and 1983.

Evaluation of the impact of the Minnesota Law has been indirect. Police officers were interviewed by Watne (1983), who found that they were encouraged to view drunk-driving patrol as more meaningful since the administrative license revocation law. Rodgers and Clearly (1983) conducted a survey of the public, revealing that 86 percent of drivers were aware of the new policies and one-fourth of those both aware of the policies and not abstainers reported that they changed their behavior in consequence. Forst Lowery, a Minnesota traffic safety official who was also a member of the Presidential Commission on Drunk Driving, claims to have found evidence for a deterrent effect of the new law in a strong correlation between the numbers of licenses revoked in Minnesota and the death rate (Lowery 1983). Although both the death rate decline and license suspension increase are impressive, the analysis is not convincing because no baseline data are presented for either series. However, the interpretation is a reasonable one. There are now eighteen separate "natural experiments" in administrative license suspension available in the United States for formal analysis in order to obtain more convincing evidence on the possible deterrent effect of this promising intervention.

Accepting Lowery's conclusion for the sake of the argument, one must recall that administrative license suspension increases certainty as well as swiftness of punishment, so the theoretical disentanglement of these two issues has not been accomplished as well as might be hoped. Indeed, such a separation may be a practical impossibility. Moreover, the Rodgers and Cleary poll found that the majority of drivers perceived that the severity of punishment had increased with the new law, thus incorporating all three variables of the deterrence proposition. If more adequate research confirms the suspicion that administrative license suspension is an effective legal countermeasure for drunk driving, the relative contribution of swiftness, certainty, and severity of punishment remain to be sorted out. However, in my opinion, added swiftness of punishment is the most notable factor differentiating administrative license suspension from other deterrence-based drunk-driving countermeasures, and an interpretation of a deterrent effect due to swiftness of punishment may be reasonable.

Conclusion

Recent experience in the United States seems to support the conclusion, reached on the basis of earlier international experience, that legal intervention intended to deter drunk drivers succeeds in the short run to the extent that it is capable of affecting drivers' perceptions of certainty of punishment. It's ability to achieve long-run results is still unknown. No important support has been found for the efficacy of measures based on increasing only the severity of punishment, and the distortions in the criminal-justice system produced by such measures have been further documented. Initial impressions of the efficacy of administrative license suspension offer some hope for the effectiveness of measures leading to increased swiftness of punishment. This evidence, however, is not yet firmly grounded and the distinction between swiftness and the other deterrence variables has not been maintained in current experience. In brief, the deterrent approach to reducing drunk driving seems capable of producing results in the short run but long-run results continue to be evasive.

These facts notwithstanding, the reports and legislative initiatives of the past few years have seldom ventured into countermeasures beyond those oriented to deterrence. This strikes me as unfortuante. Drunk driving is not the activity of a small deviant minority. Vast numbers of the public engage in it: a recent Gallup Poll commissioned by the *Wall Street Journal* found that 80 percent of American business executives admit to the offense. As a sociologist I am impressed by the evidence that drunk driving is built into our ordinary patterns of recreation and transportation. Although on the basis of present evidence the promise of deterrence may be fulfilled with vastly increased effort, a greater promise may lie with measures that strive to affect the broader patterns of drinking and driving. New York City, with its dense population and excellent public transportation, has a very small problem with drunk driving. Changes might be accomplished in communities with very different structures to produce similar results, for instance the subsidization of taxi service.

Finally, I think we must accept the prognosis that no measures will eliminate drunk driving; the best we can do will be to reduce it. Cannot steps be taken to lower the chances that a drunk driver will crash (for example, by reducing the numbers of unyielding fixed objects along our highways) or to lower the likelihood that a given crash will produce serious injury and death (for instance, by installing passive occupant restraints in all vehicles)? The problem is complex and serious, and our response must be multifaceted and versatile. Above all, we should be prepared to evaluate competently and impartially whatever we do, to abandon what does not work, and to keep on trying new approaches.

References

Gropper, B.; C. Martorama; L. Mock; M. O'Connor; and W.P. Travers. 1983. "The Impacts of Mandatory Confinement for Drunk Driving on Criminal Justice Operations (Summary Report)." Technical Report. Washington, D.C.: National Institute of Justice.

Los Angeles County Municipal Courts Planning and Research. 1983. "The 1982 Driving under the Influence Law and the Los Angeles County Municipal Courts." Memorandum. Los Angeles: County Courts.

Lowery, F. 1983. " 'Eating the Plastic—'the Minnesota Two-Track System for Drinking Driver Control: A Report on Quick Driver License Revocation Based on Alcohol Test Result, Independent of Criminal Charge or Court Outcome." Mimeographed. St. Paul, Minn.: Department of Public Safety.

Peck, R. 1983. "The Traffic Safety Impact of California's New Drunk Driving Law (AB 541): An Evaluation of the First Nine Months of Experience." Mimeographed. Sacramento: State of California Department of Motor Vehicles.

Presidential Commission on Drunk Driving. 1983. *Final Report*. Washington, D.C.: Presidential Commission.

Rodgers, A., and J. Clearly. 1983. "Evaluation of Recent Legislative Reforms Related to Drunken Driving in Minnesota: The Perceptions of Minnesota Drivers." Mimeographed. St. Paul: Minnesota House of Representatives Research Department.

Salzberg, P., and S. Paulsrude. 1983. "Legal Sanctions for Driving while Intoxicated: Effect of the 1980 Washington Law on Drunk Driving Recidivism." Mimeographed. Olympia, Wash.: Driver Services Division, Department of Licensing, Research Report No. 51.

Voas, R., and J. Hause. 1983. "Deterring the Drinking Driver: The Stockton Experience." Mimeographed. Alexandria, Va.: National Public Services Research Institute.

Watne, J. 1983. "Prehearing License Revocation of Drinking Drivers: The Minnesota Experience." Mimeographed. St. Paul, Minn.: Office of the Attorney General.

Woods, B., and R. Calderwood. 1982. "Impact Evaluation of the BAT Mobiles in Albuquerque, New Mexico." Mimeograhed. Albuquerque, N.M.: University of New Mexico Division of Government Research.

References

Andenaes, J. 1974. *Punishment and Deterrence.* Ann Arbor: University of Michigan Press.

_____ . 1978. "The Effects of Scandinavia's Drinking-and-Driving Laws." *Scandinavian Studies in Criminology* 6:35-54.

Andenaes, J., and R. Sørensen. 1979. "Alkohol og dødsulykker i trafikken." *Lov og rett* (1979):83-109.

Beitel, G.; M. Sharp; and W. Glauz. 1975. "Probability of Arrest While Driving under the Influence of Alcohol." *Journal of Studies of Alcohol* 36:237-256.

Birrell, J. 1975. "The Compulsory Breathaliser .05 Percent Legislation in Victoria." In *Alcohol, Drugs and Traffic Safety,* edited by S. Israelstam and S. Lambert. Proceedings of the Sixth International Conference on Alcohol, Drugs and Traffic Safety. Toronto: Addiction Research Foundation of Ontario.

Bjerver, K.; L. Goldberg; and P. Linde. 1955. "Blood Alcohol Levels in Hospitalized Victims of Traffic Accidents." *Proceedings of the Second International Conference on Alcohol and Road Traffic.* Toronto: Garden City Press Cooperative.

Blumenthal, M., and H. Ross. 1973. "Two Experimental Studies of Traffic Law: The Effect of Legal Sanctions on DUI Offenders and the Effect of Court Appearance on Traffic Law Violators." Technical Report DOT HS 249 2 437. Washington, D.C.: National Highway Traffic Safety Administration.

Blumstein, A.; J. Cohen; and D. Nagin, eds. 1978. *Deterrence and Incapacitation: Estimating the Effects of Criminal Sanctions on Crime Rates.* Washington, D.C.: National Academy of Sciences.

Bø; O.; J. Haffner; Ø. Langård; J. Trumpy; J. Bredesen; and P. Lunde. 1974. "Ethanol and Diazepam as Causative Agents in Road Traffic Accidents." In *Alcohol, Drugs and Traffic Safety,* edited by S. Israelstam and S. Lambert. Proceedings of the Sixth International Conference on Alcohol, Drugs and Traffic Safety. Toronto: Addiction Research Foundation of Ontario.

Bonnichsen, R., and S. Åquist. 1968. "Alkoholens Roll vid Svenska Trafikolykor." *Alkoholfrågen* 20:202-203.

Bonnichsen, R., and I. Lingmark. 1972. "Alkoholens Roll vid Trafikolykor." *Alkoholfrågen* 56:98-99.

Bonnichsen, R., and A. Solarz. 1980. "Alcohol and Road Traffic Accidents with Severe Injury to the Driver." Paper presented at the Eighth International Conference on Alcohol, Drugs and Traffic Safety, Stockholm.

Borkenstein, R. 1975. "Problems of Enforcement, Adjudication, and Sanctioning." In *Alcohol, Drugs and Traffic Safety*, edited by S. Israelstam and S. Lambert. Proceedings of the Sixth International Conference on Alcohol, Drugs and Traffic Safety. Toronto: Addiction Research Foundation of Ontario.

Boston University School of Law. 1976. " Analysis of Drivers Most Responsible for Fatal Accidents versus a Control Sample." Technical Report DOT HS-801-916. Washington, D.C.: National Highway Traffic Safety Administration.

Breitenecker, L. 1962. "The Effects of the Austrian Legislation Concerning Drunken Driving." In *Alcohol and Road Traffic: Proceedings of the Third International Conference on Alcohol and Road Traffic*. London: British Medical Association.

California Highway Patrol. 1966. *Operation 101: Final Report, Phase 1, Background and Accident Analysis*. Sacramento: California Highway Patrol.

Cameron, M.; P. Strang; and A. Vulcan. 1980. "Evaluation of Random Breath Testing in Victoria, Australia." Paper presented at the Eighth International Conference on Alcohol, Drugs and Traffic Safety, Stockholm.

Cameron, T. 1977. "Alcohol and Traffic." In *Alcohol, Casualties and Crime*, edited by M. Aarens; T. Cameron; J. Roizen; R. Roizen; R. Room; D. Schneberk; and D. Wingard. Berkeley, Calif.: Social Research Group.

Campbell, D. 1969. "Reforms as Experiments." *American Psychologist* 24:402-409.

Campbell, D., and J. Stanley. 1963. *Experimental and Quasi-Experimental Designs for Research*. Chicago: Rand McNally.

Carr, B.; H. Goldberg; and C. Farbar. 1975. "The Canadian Breathaliser Legislation: An Inferential Evaluation." In *Alcohol, Drugs and Traffic Safety*, edited by S. Israelstam and S. Lambert. Proceedings of the Sixth International Conference on Alcohol, Drugs and Traffic Safety. Toronto: Addiction Research Foundation of Ontario.

_____ . 1974. *The Breathaliser Legislation: An Inferential Evaluation*. Ottawa: Ministry of Transport.

Chambers, L; R. Roberts; and C. Voeller. 1976. "The Epidemiology of Traffic Accidents and the Effect of the 1969 Breathaliser Amendment in Canada." *Accident Analysis and Prevention* 8:201-206.

Chambliss, W. 1966. "The Deterrent Influence of Punishment." *Crime and Delinquency* 12:70-75.

Christensen, P.; S. Fosser; and A. Glad. 1978. *Drunken Driving in Norway*. Oslo: Institute of Transport Economics.

Cohen, L. 1978. "Sanction Threats and Violation Behavior: An Inquiry into Perceptual Variation." In *Quantitative Studies in Criminology*, edited by C. Wellford. Beverly Hills: Sage Publications.

Coldwell, B.B., ed 1957. *Report on Impaired Driving Tests*. Ottawa: Queen's Printer and Controller of Stationery.

Cook, P. 1979. "Research in Criminal Deterrence: Laying the Groundwork for the Second Decade." Draft manuscript.

———. 1977. "Punishment and Crime: A Critique of Current Findings Concerning the Preventive Effects of Punishment." *Law and Contemporary Problems* 41:164-204.

DeBuhan, P., and C. Filou. 1979. *L'Alcool sur la Route en 1979 et son Évolution depuis 1977: Exposé des Principaux Résultats*. Arcueil, France: ONSER.

Ennis, P. 1977. "General Deterrence and Police Enforcement: Effective Countermeasures against Drinking and Driving." *Journal of Safety Research* 9:15-23.

Erikson, K. 1966. *Wayward Puritans: A Study in the Sociology of Deviance*. New York: Wiley & Sons.

Farris, R; T. Malone; and H. Lilliefors. 1976. "A Comparison of Alcohol Involvement in Exposed and Injured Drivers. Phases I and II." Technical Report DOT HS 801 826. Washington, D.C.: National Highway Traffic Safety Administration.

Fennessy, E.; R. Borkenstein; H. Joksch; F. Leahy; and K. Joscelyn. 1968. *The Technical Content of State and Community Police Traffic Services Programs*. Hartford, Conn.: The Travelers Research Center, Inc.

Field, A. 1971. "The Drinking Driver: Chicago's Quest for a New Ethic." *Traffic Digest and Review* 19:1-6.

Fisher, E., and R. Reeder. 1974. *Vehicle Traffic Law*. Evanston, Ill.: Traffic Institute of Northwestern University.

Force, R. 1977. "The Inadequacy of Drinking-Driving Laws: A Lawyer's View." In *Proceedings of the Seventh International Conference on Alcohol, Drugs and Traffic Safety*. Canberra: Australian Government Publishing Service.

Gibbs, J. 1975. *Crime, Punishment and Deterrence*. New York: Elsevier Scientific Publishing Company.

Grasmick, H., and D. Green. 1980. "Legal Punishment, Social Disapproval, and Internalization as Inhibitors of Illegal Behavior." *Journal of Criminal Law and Criminology* 71:325-335.

Gusfield, J. 1981. *The Culture of Public Problems: Drinking-Driving and the Symbolic Order*. Chicago: University of Chicago Press.

Haddon, W., Jr. 1980. "Options for the Prevention of Motor Vehicle Crash Injury." *Israel Journal of Medical Sciences* 16:45-68.

Hansson, C. 1972. *Alkohol och läkemedel vid dodsolyckor i traffiken i södra Sverige.* Lund, Sweden: State Forensic Medical Station.

Hauge, R. 1978. "Drinking and Driving: Biochemistry, Law and Morality." *Scandinavian Studies in Criminology* 6:61-68.

Havard, J. 1977. "An International View of Legislation and Its Effect." In *Proceedings of the Seventh International Conference on Alcohol, Drugs and Traffic Safety.* Canberra: Australian Government Publishing Service.

Hoffman, L. 1973. "Alcohol and Traffic Safety: Screening Out the Drunken Driver." In *Technological Shortcuts to Social Change*, edited by A. Etzioni. New York: Russell Sage Foundation.

Hurst, P. 1978. "Blood Test Legislation in New Zealand." *Accident Analysis and Prevention* 10:287-296.

_____ . 1970. "Estimating the Effectiveness of Blood Alcohol Limits." *Behavioral Research in Highway Safety* 1:87-99.

Hurst, P., and P. Wright. 1980. "Deterrence at Last: The Ministry of Transport's Alcohol Blitzes." Paper presented at the Eighth International Conference on Alcohol, Drugs and Traffic Safety, Stockholm.

Insurance Institute for Highway Safety. 1981. *Policy Options for Reducing the Motor Vehicle Crash Injury Cost Burden.* Washington, D.C.

Jamieson, K. 1968. "Alcohol and Driving: The Breathaliser Bogey." *Medical Journal of Australia* 2:425-434.

Johnson, P.; P. Levy; and R. Voas. 1976. "A Critique of the Paper 'Statistical Evaluations of the Effectiveness of Alcohol Safety Action Projects'." *Accident Analysis and Prevention* 8:67-77.

Jones, R., and K. Joscelyn. 1978. "Alcohol and Highway Safety: A Review of the State of Knowledge." Technical Report DOT HS 803 714. Washington, D.C.: National Highway Traffic Safety Administration.

Jones, R.; K. Joscelyn; and J. McNair. 1979. "Designing a Health/Legal System: A Manual." Technical Report DOT HS 805 138. Washington, D.C.: National Highway Traffic Safety Administration.

Kates, Peat, Marwick and Co. 1970. *Awareness of the Breathaliser Legislation.* Ottawa: Ministry of Transport.

King, J., and M. Tipperman. 1975. "Offense of Driving while Intoxicated: The Development of Statutes and Case Law in New York." *Hofstra Law Review* 3:541-604.

Kelling, G., and A. Pate. 1974. *The Kansas City Preventive Patrol Experiment.* Washington, D.C.: Police Foundation.

Klein, T. 1981. "An Evaluation of the 55 MPH Speed Limit Enforcement Demonstration Projects in Connecticut and Utah." Technical Report, in draft. Washington, D.C.: National Highway Traffic Safety Administration.

Klette, H. 1978. "On the Politics of Drunken Driving in Sweden." *Scandinavian Studies in Criminology* 6:113-120.

Little, J. 1980. "Drinking, Driving and the Law." *Criminal Justice Abstracts* 12:261-288.

Lonsdale, C., and B. Stacey. 1981. *An Analysis of Drink-Driving Research in New Zealand*. Christchurch: Department of Psychology, University of Canterbury, New Zealand.

Lundevall, J., and M. Olaisen. 1976. "Alkoholpåvirkning hos Motorvognførere drept i Traffikkulykker." *Lov og Rett* (1976):271-275.

McCain, L., and R. McCleary. 1979. "Analysis of the Simple Interrupted Time Series Quasi-Experiment." In *Quasi-Experimentation: Design and Analysis Issues for Field Settings*, edited by T. Cook and D. Campbell. Chicago: Rand McNally.

McCleary, R., and R. Hay, Jr. 1980. *Applied Time Series Analysis for the Social Sciences*. Beverly Hills: Sage Publications.

McEwen, J., and J. McGuire. 1981. "Traffic Law Sanctions." Technical Report DOT HS 805 876. Washington, D.C.: National Highway Traffic Safety Administration.

Misner, R., and P. Ward. 1975. "Severe Penalties for Driving Offenses: Deterrence Analysis." *Arizona State Law Journal* (1975):677-713.

Moore, M., and D. Gerstein, eds. 1981. *Alcohol and Public Policy: Beyond the Shadow of Prohibition*. Washington, D.C.: National Academy Press.

Nichols, J.; V. Ellingstad; and D. Struckman-Johnson. 1978a. "An Experimental Evaluation of the Effectiveness of Short Term Education and Rehabilitation Programs for Convicted Drinking Drivers." Paper presented at the National Council on Alcoholism Annual Forum, St. Louis, Missouri.

Nichols, J.; E. Weinstein; V. Ellingstad; and D. Struckman-Johnson. 1978b. "The Specific Deterrence Effect of ASAP Education and Rehabilitation Programs." Paper presented at the National Safety Congress, Chicago, Illinois.

Noordzij, P. 1980. "Recent Trends in Countermeasures and Research on Drinking and Driving in the Netherlands." Paper presented at the Eighth International Conference on Alcohol, Drugs and Traffic Safety, Stockholm.

———. 1977. "The Introduction of a Statutory BAC Limit of 50mg/100ml and Its Effects on Drinking and Driving Habits and Traffic Accidents." In *Proceedings of the Seventh International Conference on Alcohol, Drugs and Traffic Safety*. Canberra: Australian Government Publishing Service.

Nordegren, T. 1981. "Alcohol and Alcoholism in Sweden." *Social Change in Sweden* (newsletter of the Swedish Information Service), no. 23, December.

Norström, T. 1978. "Drunken Driving: A Tentative Causal Model." *Scandinavian Studies in Criminology* 6:69-78.

——— . 1981. *Studies in the Causation and Prevention of Traffic Crime.* Stockholm: Almqvist and Wiksell International.

OECD Road Research Group. 1978. *New Research on the Role of Alcohol and Drugs in Road Accidents.* Paris.

——— . 1974. *Research on Traffic Law Enforcement: Effects of the Enforcement of Legislation on Road User Behavior and Traffic Accidents.* Paris.

Packer, H. 1968. *The Limits of the Criminal Sanction.* Stanford, Calif.: Stanford University Press.

Parsons, K. 1978. *Violence on the Road: A Logical Extension to the Subculture of Violence Thesis?* Research Section, Department of Justice, Wellington, New Zealand.

Persson, L. 1978. "Actual Drunken Driving in Sweden." *Scandinavian Studies in Criminology* 6:101-112.

Reigstad, A.; J. Bredesen; and P. Lunde. 1977. *Ulykker, Alkohol og Nervemedesin, Førekomst og Samvariasjon.* Oslo: Universiteitsforlaget.

Ringkjøb, R.; and I. Lereim. 1977. "Hodeskader og Alkohol, et Klinisk og Statistisk Materiale far Trondheimsomradet." Unpublished manuscript.

Robertson, L.; R. Rich; and H. Ross. 1973. "Jail Sentences for Driving while Intoxicated in Chicago: A Judicial Policy that Failed." *Law and Society Review* 8:55-67.

Ross, H. 1979. "Blood Alcohol Concentrations among Traffic Fatalities in Inner North London: A Research Note." *Medicine, Science and Law* 19:233-234.

——— . 1977. "Deterrence Regained: The Cheshire Constabulary's 'Breathalyser Blitz'." *Journal of Legal Studies* 6:241-249.

——— . 1976. "The Neutralization of Severe Penalties: Some Traffic Law Studies." *Law and Society Review* 10:403-413.

——— . 1975. "The Scandinavian Myth: The Effectiveness of Drinking-and-Driving Legislation in Sweden and Norway." *Journal of Legal Studies* 4:285-310.

——— . 1973. "Law, Science and Accidents: The British Road Safety Act of 1967." *Journal of Legal Studies* 2:1-78.

Ross, H., and M. Blumenthal. 1975. "Some Problems in Experimentation in a Legal Setting." *American Sociologist* 10:150-155.

Ross, H.; R. McCleary; and T. Epperlein. 1982. "Deterrence of Drinking and Driving in France: An Evaluation of the Law of July 12, 1978." *Law and Society Review*, forthcoming.

Sabey, B. 1978. "A Review of Drinking and Drug-Taking in Road Accidents in Great Britain." Paper presented to the American Association of Automotive Medicine and the International Association for Accident and Traffic Medicine, Ann Arbor, Michigan.

Sabey, B., and P. Codling. 1975. "Alcohol and Road Accidents in Great Britain." In *Alcohol, Drugs and Traffic Safety*, edited by S. Israelstam and S. Lambert. Proceedings of the Sixth International Conference on Alcohol, Drugs and Traffic Safety. Toronto: Addiction Research Foundation of Ontario.

Saunders, A. 1975. "Seven Years Experience of Blood-Alcohol Limits in Britain." In *Alcohol, Drugs and Traffic Safety*, edited by S. Israelstam and S. Lambert. Proceedings of the Sixth International Conference on Alcohol, Drugs and Traffic Safety. Toronto: Addiction Research Foundation of Ontario.

Shumate, R. 1961. *Effect of Increased Patrol on Accidents, Diversion and Speed*. Evanston, Ill.: Northwestern University Traffic Institute.

Smart, R. 1972. "Observation of Tavern Patrols before and after the Compulsory Breath Test Law in Canada." *Quarterly Journal of Alcohol Studies* 33:1122-1128.

Snortum, J. 1981. "Drinking-and-Driving in Norway and Sweden: Another Look at 'the Scandinavian myth'." Draft manuscript.

SOU (Statens Offentliga Utredningar). 1970. *Trafiknykterhetsbrott*, 61. Government documents, Stockholm.

Summers, L., and D. Harris. 1978. "The General Deterrence of Driving while Intoxicated. Volume I: System Analysis and Computer-Based Simulation." Technical Report DOT HS 803 582. Washington, D.C.: National Highway Traffic Safety Administration.

Surell, V. n.d. "The Importance of General Prevention in the Combating of Drunken Driving." Mimeographed.

SWOV (Institute for Road Safety Research). 1977. *Drinking by Motorists*. Voorburg, Netherlands.

_____ . 1969. *Alcohol and Road Safety: Countermeasures and Research*. Voorburg, Netherlands.

Tittle, C. 1980. *Sanctions and Social Deviance: The Question of Deterrence*. New York: Praeger Publishers.

Tobias, J. 1968. *Crime and Industrial Society in the 19th Century*. New York: Shocken Books.

U.S. Department of Transportation. 1980. "A Report to the Congress on the Effect of Motorcycle Helmet Use Law Repeal—A Case for Helmet Use. Technical Report DOT HS 805 312. Washington, D.C.: National Highway Traffic Safety Administration.

_____ . 1979a. *Alcohol and Highway Safety Laws: A National Overview*. Washington, D.C.: National Highway Traffic Safety Administration.

_____ . 1979b. *Alcohol Safety Action Projects Evaluation of Operations: Data, Tables of Results and Formulation.* Washington, D.C.: National Highway Traffic Safety Administration.

_____ . 1968. "Alcohol and Highway Safety." Report to the U.S. Congress. Washington, D.C.

Van Ooijen, D. 1977. "The Effects of a New DWI Law." In *Proceedings of the Seventh International Conference on Alcohol, Drugs and Driving.* Canberra: Australian Government Publishing Service.

Vingilis, E., and L. Salutin. 1980. "A Prevention Programme for Drinking Driving." *Accident Analysis and Prevention* 12:267-274.

Vogt, I. 1980. Draft manuscript on German literature on alcohol, casualties and crime. Berkeley, Calif.: Social Research Group.

Votey, H. 1978. "The Deterrence of Drunken Driving in Norway and Sweden: An Econometric Analysis of Existing Policies." *Scandinavian Studies in Criminology* 6:79-100.

Wagenaar, A. 1981. "Effects of the Raised Legal Drinking Age on Motor Vehicle Accidents in Michigan." *HSRI Research Review* 11:1-8.

Waller, J. 1971. "Factors Associated with Police Evaluation of Drinking in Fatal Highway Crashes." *Journal of Safety Research* 3:35-41.

Williams, A.; P. Zador; S. Harris; and R. Karpf. 1982. "The Effect of Raising the Legal Minimum Drinking Age on Fatal Crash Involvement." *Journal of Legal Studies,* forthcoming.

Wilson, J. 1975. *Thinking About Crime.* New York: Basic Books.

Zador, P. 1976. "Statistical Evaluation of the Effectiveness of 'Alcohol Safety Action Projects'." *Accident Analysis and Prevention* 8:51-66.

_____ . 1977. "A Rejoinder to a Critique of the Paper 'Statistical Evaluation of the Effectiveness of Alcohol Safety Action Projects' by Johnson et al." *Accident Analysis and Prevention* 9:15-19.

_____ . 1978. "Review of Two Papers by H.L. Votey on Law Enforcement and Drunken Drivers." Privately circulated memorandum.

Zimring, F. 1978. "Policy Experiments in General Deterrence: 1970-1975." In *Deterrence and Incapacitation: Estimating the Effects of Criminal Sanctions on Crime Rates,* edited by A. Blumstein; J. Cohen; and D. Nagin. Washington, D.C.: National Academy of Sciences.

Zimring, F. and G. Hawkins. 1973. *Deterrence: The Legal Threat in Crime Control.* Chicago: University of Chicago Press.

Zylman, R. 1975. "DWI Enforcement Programs: Why Are They Not More Effective?" *Accident Analysis and Prevention* 7:179-190.

_____ . 1974. "Semantic Gymnastics on Alcohol-Highway Crash Research." *Journal of Alcohol and Drug Education* 19:7-23.

Index

133

About the Author

H. Laurence Ross is professor of sociology and Chair, Department of Sociology, at the University of New Mexico. He was educated at Swarthmore College and Harvard University. His academic career has included, in addition to posts at several U.S. universities, a Fulbright lectureship at the Catholic University of Louvain, Belgium, and a visiting fellowship at the Centre for Socio-Legal Studies, Oxford University, England. His chief professional interest is the sociology of law. He is author of *Settled Out of Court: A Sociological Study of Insurance Claims Adjustment* and editor of *Law and Deviance*. His long-standing interest in the contributions of studies in traffic law to sociology and criminology has resulted in numerous articles. Professor Ross has served as the director of the Program in Law and Social Sciences at the National Science Foundation and trustee of the Law and Society Association. He is currently secretary of the Society for the Study of Social Problems and editor of the *Law and Policy Quarterly*.